# Mad Dogs, Dreamers and Sages

## Growth in the Age of Ideas

# Mad Dogs, Dreamers and Sages

## Growth in the Age of Ideas

Stephen Zades and Jane Stephens

ELOUNDA
PRESS

*For Bonnie & Alex, who make life worth writing about.*

*To  Katherine, Stamos, Helen and Lainie for lifetimes of love.*

*–Stephen Zades*

*To Julie, John, Jean and Jim—the mad dogs, dreamers and sages I grew up with.*

*–Jane Stephens*

Published by Elounda Press. www.eloundapress.com

*Grateful acknowledgement is made for permission to reprint the article by Stephen H. Zades and Jane Stephens, "Creativity Regained" as first published in Inc. magazine September, 2003, reprinted by permission of Gruner+Jahr USA Publishing.*

**Library of Congress Cataloging-in-Publication Data:**
Zades, Stephen and Stephens, Jane
Mad Dogs, dreamers and sages: organizational growth in the age of ideas
Library of Congress Number: 2003110882

ISBN 0-9744073-0-5

Book cover original watercolor painting and design by Fu-Ding Cheng

Printed in the United States of America

FIRST EDITION

10 9 8 7 6 5 4 3 2 1

# Contents

# Preface

The genesis of this journey is a personal one. I had just finished six exhilarating years as a CEO building a successful advertising agency…an idea company that lived and thrived by the strength of its ability to create. Not just once in awhile, but all the time. The feeling was electric, like opening night every day. I could see the exponential potential of real growth through innovation.

As I set out to explore the dynamics of growth through innovation, I had no intention of writing a book, but that's where my passions carried me. I believe creating real, sustainable growth is the number one imperative for leaders today.

**Creating real, sustainable growth is the number one imperative.**

The challenge of how to grow an organization and fully develop the talents of its people has always inspired me. Despite massive cost-cutting, financial engineering, and creative accounting, companies everywhere are struggling. They seem unable to create real, sustainable, top-line growth. More importantly, they seem to have forgotten that people are the very source of innovation itself. Has the landscape fundamentally changed? Are we losing the ability to grow inventively?

Early on in this project, I had the good fortune to meet Jane Stephens. At that point, what I knew for sure was that real growth ideas for business would need to come from new places. I had decided to take to the open road to experience the nutrient-rich environments of innovators who had piqued my curiosity. Jane turned out to be the perfect partner for analyzing my exploration of uncharted territory. As a writing teacher, she had cultivated thousands of moments of individual discovery and leaps of imagination—the *Aha!*s that erupt as students break through old limits and into new ways of thinking.

Like climbers planning a difficult first assent, we spent hours at Borders and Starbucks conceptualizing the terrain. We soon realized the sheer scope of the project would require the resources of both of us; it was going to be a long-term mission! By then, we were both hooked, and we made the commitment to see the journey through.

The first year was full-throttle. I cashed in thousands of frequent flyers to interview innovators in different fields. As Jane and I pored over the material I brought back from the road, we began to see two different veins of research. The first was the kind of immediate and visceral understanding that can only be had from direct contact with primary sources. Through my face-to-face work with innovators we were able to see the distinct qualities and strategies each was bringing to their discreet fields. The second vein was more abstract. By bringing together the intellectual breakthroughs of diverse and unfamiliar fields, we began to see new trans-disciplinary approaches to growth. The depth of the personal, experiential research fueled the wide-ranging breadth of the "big picture" research.

During the second year of the project, the going got harder. The multiplicity of connections was staggering, and the possibilities for arranging our material seemed limitless. We traveled, talked, and read widely. We took turns breaking trail, expanding our scope of innovators, and discovering critical distinctions within our central question. But we kept bringing it back to base camp with this question: What can we learn about genuine, sustainable growth?

Other than this fascination with genuine growth and an audacious confidence that we could translate it across disciplines, industries, and generations, Jane and I had very little in common when we set out. We had each worked in a wide-range of contexts in our own fields, but these are fields that don't often collide—or collude.

A New Yorker with an MBA, a wife, and a three-year-old, I spent twenty years as an executive in the field of marketing and advertising. From basic training at Procter & Gamble to the Wild West of Madison Avenue, I've worked with top Fortune 500 companies as well as wily entrepreneurial start-ups.

Jane hails from the Midwest and earned her Ph.D. in the South. She has a classroom, a husband, six kids, and twenty years of experience as an English teacher. She has taught writing, history, and literature in a variety of contexts, from high schools in Indiana and colleges in Kenya to universities in North Carolina.

**Innovation involves complex forces— collaboration, struggle, and timing.**

Our diverse backgrounds served us well as we undertook a study for which we had no models, no established methodology, and no common language. We realized that studying growth across business and academe would be a challenge—like studying physics in Japanese. And we expected that some of the fineness would be lost in the process. But here's the surprise: the research and the translation became equal partners in our learning. We didn't study growth in one field and then translate it to another; rather, we created a sort of third language. The translation expanded our sense of understanding.

We had no choice but to innovate, to create something new. At every level, whether cosmic, organizational, or individual, innovation involves complex forces—collaboration, struggle, and timing. Real learning, like real growth, is inherently disorderly. It happens in spurts and stutters, usually when we're not looking. We do our best to organize, arrange, and pay attention, but the puppies never get born in the basket—or at the appointed time. Nonetheless, we can get better at recognizing the signs, preparing the places, and understanding the process.

That is exactly what happened as our project unfolded. We developed sensitivity to the phenomenon of growth and to the many opportunities we all miss to cultivate it in our public and private lives.

So the tasks of gathering, sifting, interpreting, and connecting the work and insights of our mad dogs, dreamers, and sages took place against the backdrop of a flow of interpretation—from education to business, from theory to practice, from production to curriculum, from individual to corporate.

Significantly, we each brought to this collaboration an array of other voices. In addition to the subjects of our interviews, this project is peopled by the wise and diverse voices we brought from our own fields and experiences—mine from business and the arts, and Jane's from teaching and her travels.

And we have brought along the people who shaped us—my vivacious musician mother and soft-spoken, wise Greek father; Jane's extravagant, entrepreneurial father and imaginative mother; first-person mentors like Sue Henry and Phil Hanes, and the second-hand ones we've gleaned from our travels.

And then there are those who have faithfully walked alongside us—my spunky wife, Jane's unflappable husband, our brothers, sisters, colleagues, clients, and students, as well as sons and daughters of both the adolescent and toddler variety who continually re-loaded our dice, supplying the urgency and stretching the meaning of the conversation. Like all good talks with kindred spirits, there's no end to the stretching—even as we have our hand on the door to leave. Why is it that the best questions always come in the last ten minutes of class, and the best ideas just before the shipping date?

–Stephen H. Zades

*******

When I was 23, I spent two years in Kenya teaching school in the fertile highlands along the edge of the Great Rift Valley. During the long breaks between school terms, I would load extra jerry tins of water and fuel onto the old Land Cruiser I'd bought from the Norwegian Embassy and drive up into the Northern Frontier District.

Driving north toward Lake Turkana, the Jade Sea, I would camp along the way, traveling off-road much of the time, and sleeping on the roof of the Land Cruiser at night. Some nights I'd be awakened by the drums and singing of young Samburu morans and some mornings by the bellowing of feuding elephants. What struck me during these journeys was that the terrain was totally unmappable.

Roads and rivers, the usual markers of physical maps, were in constant flux, and directions were given in terms of tribal areas. *Drive north and once you cross the river and get into Samburu country, start looking for the station. But keep in mind, the road may peter out and the river might be dry.* How would you recognize Samburu country? By things that had more permanence than rivers—their language and homes, the ways the mothers carried their babies and how the children waved from the roadside.

The area was still profoundly tribal: one village spoke Samburu and lived off their cows; the next spoke Kikuyu and lived off potatoes. To the Samburu, eating something that grew from the ground was subhuman, an animal act; for the Kikuyu, drinking warm milk and cow's blood was abhorrent. Although, from my perspective, both groups were more alike than distinctive. The Kikuyu had so defined themselves as being not-Samburu and the Samburu had so defined themselves as being not-Kikuya that much of their language and values seemed organized around the distinction.

I must have staggered their imagination. I was neither one tribe nor the other. Njroge, my Kikuyu language teacher, explained that I was neither a *mwanake* (man) nor a *mutumia* (woman), I was a *murutani* (teacher). Even harder to take was the question of my status as human. The Kikuyu word for human is *mugikuyu* (one who is Kikuyu). He apologetically explained that I was *MwAmerik*. Not even a real word, a hybrid between human and American. In order to name me as human, he had to invent new language. But, because I existed between the cracks of their categories, I was indulged, even welcomed.

Those were good days in eastern Africa. It was the late seventies; Kenya was fifteen years into independence and still untouched by the devastation of AIDS within the country and terrorism from abroad. I loved the tribalism I saw at that time; from my perspective it was rich and varied and exotic. But in the past two decades, tribalism has scourged the continent.

With the influx of new communication, weapons, and organization, tribalism has become increasingly deadly. In Rwanda half a million Tutsis were killed by Hutus in 1994; and in Congo, a quarter of a million Hutus were slaughtered by Tutsis in 2002. These weren't people with unfamiliar customs who raided each other from great distances; these were neighbors who lived and worked together everyday—in the same fields, communities, and families. Tribalism had rendered them unable to see each other's humanity, evidence that the same traditions that support culture, commerce and growth in stable times can wreak vast destruction in times of great change.

The truth is that all of us have a preservational instinct towards tribalism. We are living in an era of cataclysmic change, and our tendency is to insulate. When we feel uncertain, we tend to narrow our language and live in tighter realities. We define ourselves against competing dualities: you don't meet an English teacher, you meet a compositionist or a literary scholar; you don't meet a lawyer, you meet a corporate attorney or a litigator. And you can distinguish between them because they dress differently, speak a different language, and are disgusted by each other's habits.

We have become less indulgent of the unfamiliar and less welcoming to difference. As our world spins faster and its people collide more often, the results of this counter-force of territorialism and specialization is increasingly unproductive and dangerous.

More than any other trend in our time, it is this trend toward narrowness, this inclination to hunker in and separate, that most threatens our ability to stay alive. The new universe we live in is quantum. It's not about dualities: true or false, pro or con, paper or plastic. It's about the spaces in between: the flows, connections, and networks. The power of the flows cannot be discovered through a dulling of the individual parts or the mass dilution of language, custom, and habit. The Wal-Mart minimalism that has rendered every exit on every interstate highway in America identical is inhospitable to real variety and exchange.

The growth of vigorous individuals and organizations comes not from their ability to narrow the genius of their respective fields, but to move it, to translate it, and to connect it. Our two-year project has given us a window into new possibilities for fluency in an increasingly diverse world—a fluency that comes not so much from collecting what we need when the recipe calls for it, but from living and working in environments that cultivate variety, change, and exchange in ongoing ways.

I returned to Kenya in the eighties and lived there for three more years. This time with three small children, I stayed home and taught English in the local hospital. My days of great safaris and exotic adventure seemed over. But an odd thing happened.

The plumbing in our house was simple. The water from our kitchen sink flowed through a hole in the wall into our yard before trickling down into the Rift Valley below, carrying a few leftovers with it.

Soon a row of volunteer tomatoes, corn and beans began to grow along the trail of our dishwater. First, little dikdiks, the tiniest of the African antelopes would come early in the morning to nibble outside my window. Later, the local children would come to try to capture the dikdiks; then, later still, the mothers would come to collect their children. It gave me lots of opportunity to trade vegetables and to practice my Kikuyu with the village women. Over time, my dishwater had created a veritable Fertile Crescent of activity, exchange, learning, and growth.

One way to stretch ourselves is to go out of our natural habitat—to make the *chosen sojourn,* a long-held tradition for many cultures. The journey to a distant country to try one's mettle and bring back learning was a critical part of the formation of character for medieval nobility—a practice shared by Islamic, Native American, and other cultures.

**Over time, my dishwater had created a veritable Fertile Crescent**

For good and for ill, these pilgrims left their mark upon the world. They returned, not only with the knowledge they found in relics and scrolls, but with the stories that clung to their imagination and tongues like briars from the roadside. The real treasure they gathered came, not from their conquests or their scheming, but from their conversations at the crossroads.

The world is smaller now, though in some ways harder to transverse. There are no gold nuggets lying around or buffalo grazing at the next bend. And we cannot expect to find our fortune by plundering someone else's field.

But knowledge lies everywhere, more abundant and diverse than ever before. It is still to be found at the crossroads—and the crossroads are everywhere. Discovering, harvesting, translating, and engaging knowledge is no longer a function of place or even of fortune. It is geography of the mind—available to individuals and organizations. It is the domain of imaginative intelligence.

–Jane Stephens

# Introduction

*Imagine that you enter a parlor. You come late. When you arrive, others have long preceded you, and they are engaged in a heated discussion, a discussion too heated for them to pause and tell you exactly what it is about. In fact, the discussion had already begun long before any of them got there, so that no one present is qualified to retrace for you all the steps that had gone before. You listen for a while, until you decide that you have caught the tenor of the argument; then you put in your oar.*

—Kenneth Burke

In writing this book we are putting in our oar. We believe that the conversation in business today needs a serious pull in a new direction. We hope to challenge old currents of conventional organizational wisdom that are no longer moving us in generative directions. After years of merger mania, scandal, cost-cutting, and a dominant short-term mentality, we seem to have forgotten how to create real growth. We've gone as far as we can go by pushing old ideas harder in the same direction. We need to get back to the kitchen, see what we can do with what we have—and we need to discover new sources for creating what we don't have. We need to rethink the way we think, re-imagine the way we imagine. We need new ideas.

The well is dry. We are in serious need of inventive and imaginative individuals—philosophers, artists, and scientists, but we also need good businesses. Our contemporary understanding of business growth through real innovation seems underdeveloped. Attempting to reduce the dynamics of innovation to a tidy system of clichés, best practices, or easy-to-digest formulae is antithetical to the very nature of real growth. We need businesses with the imagination and intelligence to see what scientists, artists, and dreamers are seeing and to put those visions to work. We need businesses that can develop fertile environments for the Age of Ideas—an Amazon rainforest where new species can flourish.

# Imaginative Intelligence in the Age of Ideas

Part I

# 1
# Growth
# in the Age of Ideas

*If you're not busy being born, you're busy dying.*

–Bob Dylan

*The most notable distinction between living and inanimate things is that the former maintain themselves by renewal . . . As long as [a living thing] endures, it struggles to use surrounding energies in its own behalf. It uses light, air, moisture, and the material of soil. To say that it uses them is to say that it turns them into means of its own conservation. As long as it is growing, the energy it expends in thus turning the environment to account is more than compensated for by the return it gets: it grows.*

–John Dewey

This book is about the real possibility and the urgent need to create genuine sustainable growth in organizations. It is about staying alive the only way any living organism can do so—by growing. America's products are getting lighter in weight, moving first from iron ore and timber, then to smoke stack and assembly line product, and now to microprocessors and "content" spurred on by the biological, information technology, and digital revolutions.

The knowledge economy is here, and it affects all of us. Regardless of industry or profession, future value will come from the capacity to originate, innovate, and translate new ideas, organizations, markets, processes, and services.

There is an audible buzz around individuals or organizations that are actively growing. You can sense it. For our ancestors it was probably the smell of roasting game after the hunt or the sound of corn being poured onto the threshing floor. Today it might be the laughter of a birthday party, the high-fiving of the new basketball champs, the boisterous first count of receipts after a great opening day, the grand music of graduation, the birth of a new ad campaign, the completion of a deal, a breakthrough in the lab. Growing is the shared sigh of relief after a project goes to press, a baby goes to sleep, the last page of a book is turned. It is something to celebrate, something to get up for in the morning, something to organize our lives around.

**Suddenly the soil is softer, the air is cooler, and you sense that anything could grow there.**

You've known palpable moments of renewal in your own organization, or classroom, or family. They are the times when everything comes together better than any one could have hoped. There is a sense of atmospheric shift in the moments—like walking into a fern forest on a hot summer day. Suddenly the soil is softer, the air is cooler, and you sense that anything could grow there.

You follow the ferns, knowing there must be underground springs in the area and soon you come to the place where the water emerges. It's a little gurgle at this point, not the mighty river it will be by the time it gets to the sea, but pure, clear, rich, and constant. You've found the headwaters.

Speaking from your ancestors' deep sense of survival, you turn to your partner and say, "We've found it. These are the headwaters. Let's make camp here."

We believe the headwaters of growth for the Age of Ideas have been lost beneath a fury of artificial financial engineering, flow charts that don't flow, and growth plans that don't grow. In our frenzy to produce the illusion of growth, too many companies have relied on serial acquisitions, aggressive accounting practices, and financial revenue-boosting techniques, rather than the innovation of genuinely new markets, products, and services.

The failure to innovate in business, despite tremendous effort and huge cost, is abysmal. Sure, all companies are continually re-packaging to manage their constituents. Everyone knows it's too dangerous not to say things like "Innovation is our life force!" But in most companies today innovation happens, if it happens at all, only by exception or by accident.

## Organized breakdown

When we began to search out genuine sources of innovation at the beginning of our study in the spring of 2001, the terrain was pretty barren—and it got worse: Enron, WorldCom, Tyco, Global Crossing, Adelphia, AOL/Time Warner. They were falling like dead trees, exposing roots that were alarmingly frail. What's more, their falls seemed to paralyze an already skeptical market. Everywhere, growth was collapsing; companies were slowing down, shifting into reverse, pressing the pause button. There were plenty of short-term stimulants, but the effect wore out fast.

Everyday new revelations of artificial financial engineering and revenue boosting techniques came to light—off-shore accounts, off-balance-sheet entries, wire transfers, roundtrip financing, stock options, recurring special charges, inflating pension earnings…Even when the ecomony began recovering and the stock market began to rally after almost three years of decline, and the earnings appeared to be trending positively, the growth of real value was shallow. David Bianco, accounting analyst at USB in

New York says, "The quality of earnings for the S&P 500, from an accounting standpoint, is the worst it has been in more than a decade."[1] The magic show of numbers in the stock market isn't over yet.

The biggest illusion of growth, the kind to which corporations have become chillingly addicted, has come from acquisitions, mergers, and consolidations. M&A, a high risk strategy which must be deployed with great caution, has become dangerously commonplace, like a nuclear weapon in the hands of rogue operators. Too often it is a strategy of management desperation and obfuscation; and the failure rate is extraordinarily high.

> **The biggest illusion of growth, the kind to which corporations have become chillingly addicted, has come from acquisitions, mergers, and consolidations.**

An October 2002 analysis by *BusinessWeek* demonstrates the "merger hangovers" wrought by these kinds of acquisitions: of the thousand deals worth $500 million or more announced between July 1, 1995 and August 31, 2001, 61% of the buyers destroyed shareholder wealth. We've spawned a generation of CEOs that *BusinessWeek* calls *compulsive dealmakers*. And they are making bad deals, overestimating cost savings and underestimating the real cost to employee retention, sales force energy, and corporate culture. What's more, the frantic energy of the deals masks the desperate moves of these merger junkies. As *BusinessWeek* put it, "Constant changes make it hard for outsiders to follow what's going on in a company. Worse yet, there's a veritable cookbook of legal ways to play with the timing and accounting of a merger."[2]

There is no shortage of packaging tricks and short-term fixes, but sooner or later we've got to water the roots and stop painting the leaves green. As the analysts who are licking their wounds are saying about WorldCom, "They just ran out of things to buy, they couldn't keep it up." The hangover is hauntingly familiar. No matter how big the company after a merger blitz, when the curtain comes up on Oz, there's just a shoddy amplifier and a frightened guy pulling levers—or packing his getaway bag for the trip out.

## Have we forgotten how to grow?

So where's the real magic? Have our wells run dry? Where have the innovators gone?

We believe that the creative spirits are still among us and within us; muffled, discouraged, and all but suffocated by a cloying layer of scandal, bureaucracy, and cost-cutting. It is the strategic imperative and moral responsibility of leaders today to uncover, restore, and revitalize their organization's imaginative resources.

This is the Age of Ideas, and we need a new means for imagining it. We need a holistic understanding of the complexity and rich dynamics of innovation. We need to see growth as a creative process, not an accounting practice. We need to reconceive how ideas and innovation can be sustainably fostered, not stultified, by our organizations. We need to cultivate imaginative intelligence in ourselves, our organizations, and our communities.

We need to *re-member* our sources of originality, putting misplaced atrophied and engorged parts back into perspective and reconnecting with enduring sources of inspiration. As Nobel-prize winning novelist Toni Morrison writes in *The Site of Memory:*

> The act of imagination is bound up with memory. You know, they straightened out the Mississippi River in places, to make room for houses and livable acreage. Occasionally the river floods these places. "Floods" is the word

they use, but in fact it is not flooding; it is remembering. Remembering where it used to be. All water has a perfect memory and is forever trying to get back to where it was. Writers are like that: remembering where we were, what valley we ran through, what the banks were like, the light that was there and the route back to our original place. It is emotional memory—what the nerves and the skin remember as well as how it appeared. And a rush of imagination is our flooding.[3]

### Getting smarter

Whether you are in the entertainment, sunscreen, or ceiling fan business, or if you work in the arts, education, or medicine, your work is getting more complex. Like algebra equations at the end of the semester, the variables are becoming greater than the constants.

All of us, whether we drive the bus or run the company, will find the greatest variability in our future work coming from our capacity to access knowledge and use it inventively. Yet our understanding of the relationship between organizational growth and the productivity of knowledge workers in the Age of Ideas is in its infancy.

In the wake of the Industrial Age, the need for industrial workers continues to shrink, just as the need for farmers shrank as the era began. The new demand will be for knowledge workers. This will not be an easy transition. According to Peter Drucker:

> The great majority of new jobs will require qualifications the industrial worker does not possess and is poorly equipped to acquire. They require a good deal of formal education and the ability to acquire and to apply

theoretical and analytical knowledge. They require a different approach to work and a different mind-set. Above all, they require a habit of continuous learning. Displaced industrial workers thus cannot simply move into knowledge work or services the way displaced farmers and domestic workers moved into industrial work.[4]

This is an important shift for knowledge workers, but it is also important for more traditional jobs, all of which will be affected by the proliferation of knowledge—and exponentially true for those who will be leading, managing, and developing the knowledge age.[5]

With his characteristic vision, Drucker first coined the term *knowledge worker* in 1959. The new landscape he predicted has arrived, bringing with it a host of implications. Education will become the center of the knowledge society, but it will no longer be considered something we do until we are 16 or 18 or 22. Nor will learning be something we do only in schools or with teachers or through books—though it will certainly include all those things. We must reconceive learning as an ongoing and transformative process, individually and organizationally. The idea of a "terminal" degree, guaranteeing lifetime proficiency in a profession, is already obsolete.

**Learning will become, not a preparation for work, but an integral part of the work itself.**

Learning will become, not a preparation for work, but an integral part of the work itself. It will be happening all the time, and so will work. In an industrial economy, one knew if he was at work or not. Work happened in measurable ways in space and time then, but the output of the knowledge worker is much harder to locate or measure. It is never over, nor is it predictable or easily measured. In a knowledge economy, you might be hired for the number of your hours or for the depth or precision of your knowledge.

In short, all of the systems and exchanges we've derived to hire, govern, assess, and account for work are fast becoming irrelevant. But, as of yet, we have no good alternatives. Our management tools are based on the fixed elements of mass production: hours, shifts, raw materials, product, or quality. For most of us those unreplenishable elements are stretched as thin as they can reach. Stretching them further will seriously impact the world's ecosystem.

## Breaking the 80/20 rule

The good news is that real breakthroughs in the area of managing knowledge may delimit the obvious barriers to growth. None of us feel we can afford to spend more time, money, or employee hours to expand our understanding, but the truth is that all of us need to get smarter. What will that process look like? Online learning, in-service training, MBA programs, continuing education courses for specialized fields? Maybe.

But those kinds of learning draw from the same economies of time and talent as our already stretched human resources. They simply add pieces to our cobbled-together notion of on-the-job learning. The specialized will get more specialized, and one kind of new learning will be situated further and further from another kind of new learning. The compartmentalization of knowledge will become deeper and more entrenched. The result will perpetuate the ineffectual 80/20 system to which we have resigned ourselves and around which we have organized our companies.

Most of us already work in places where we accept as a given a kind of natural law that 20% of the people do 80% of the work; or, conversely, that 80% of the ideas, insights, and real productivity come from 20% of the people. In a knowledge economy, this demoralizing concept is the productivity millstone that will drown us. Because it translates into 20% of the people controlling 80% of the material, it is a disastrous model.

We urgently need to figure out how to reverse and ultimately explode the 80/20 rule. To stretch others and ourselves in new ways, we need to re-conceive the ways we grow, and in a knowledge economy much of this stretch will come from our understanding of how learning grows.

The shift to a knowledge economy has been in some ways as violent as any shift the world has known: displacing jobs, opening up vast spheres of litigation, and furthering the already disastrous social divides between old and young, haves and have-nots, urban and rural, high techs and no techs. But it has the ultimate potential to bring great benefit to everyone.

If learning and its inventive application is the main part of a knowledge worker's job—that is, the thing one brings to it, takes away from it, and has more of when the job is over than when it began—a knowledge worker has a more dynamic economic relationship with the employer than ever before. At best, the company is no longer buying the hours and energies that she would otherwise be investing in her own interests, it is growing her interests. Working, like going to school, should get more interesting as it goes along, because the individual is bringing more to the exchange—and taking more away. The knowledge economy gives workers an immense capacity for bringing a fuller sense of ownership to their work.

Why doesn't this exchange work better—in work or school? Why don't knowledge workers have an endless run of growth and pleasure and corporate profitability? Because just as our organizational infrastructures with their emphasis on rigid performance and specialization tend to stall out at a certain point, so do our educational assumptions. No one can challenge the enormous leaps of achievement America has made on every front since her inception, in science, medicine, standard of living, production, art, and knowledge. We have grown—stunningly, boisterously, and generously. But the challenge of sustainable growth requires a new level of attention to the creative process. Our traditional formulas are rooted in an agrarian age and have been modified for an industrial one. They are inadequate for the problems of the Age of Ideas. Our development of ways of representing knowledge and its variations in the organization are as rudimentary as cave paintings compared to the digital camera, and fall far short of reproducing the capacity of the human mind.

## Ecotonic times: disruption and creation

To borrow a term from biology, we are living in particularly ecotonic times. *Ecotonic* areas are those where multiple streams converge, bringing with them such a variety of elements where that balance is disrupted and a whole new ecosystem is born. Rather than resist, we must embrace ecotonic opportunity as a new paradigm in the Age of Ideas.

In clinging to an industrial mindset, we end up threatening the corporation's ability to sustain vital growth. If we remain perpetually unprepared and off-balance for the rapid shifts and surprises of multiple currents, we may miss the greatest gift of these times. This gift is the flow of contradiction and change that insures the very sustainability and reliability of innovation itself.

As change becomes the dominant certainty, organizations will increasingly have to develop the competing muscles of focus and range. This is akin to the yin/yang relationship between core values and ongoing change that Jim Collins talks about in his book *Built to Last*. After an extensive study of eighteen highly successful corporations, Collins credits their success to the visionary practice of challenging "the tyranny of the *or*" with "the genius of the *and*." He quotes F. Scott Fitzgerald who wrote, "The test of a first-rate intelligence is the ability to hold two opposed ideas in the mind at the same time, and still retain the ability to function."[6]

Whether an organization can theoretically hold two opposing ideas in tension is open to dispute, but technically speaking, an intelligent individual cannot. The human mind can only focus on one thing at a time. For instance, when we are talking on a cell phone while driving, we are focusing on either the road or the conversation. The reason we get away with doing both (most of the time) is that we have the ability to switch our focus back and forth in little micro-moves of adaptation as either the road or the conversation becomes urgent. We do it so easily that we have the illusion of focusing on both at the same time. When we are tired or scared or overloaded—or startled by something different from familiar patterns—we can lose our fluency and fail to make those critical corrections. In an idea economy, where dealing with multiple bodies of data and perspectives is the norm, the key test of first-rate intelligence will be agility, not simply the ability to hold multiple ideas at the same time, but the ability to shuttle fluently between them. The test of first-rate leaders will be their management of the spaces in between silos of knowledge.

> **The test of first-rate leaders will be their management of the spaces in between silos of knowledge.**

We have to come to grips with the ways the industrial mindset has altered the entire geography of the growth enterprise. In many ways, America's pioneer farming culture was more entrepreneurial and required a greater range of resourcefulness than the industrial society. The development of mass production narrowed the range of tasks and understanding for which any one organization or individual was responsible. Innovation became increasingly divorced from implementation.

The achievements of American industry over the last century and a half have been staggering. Peter Drucker attributes this to our capacity to focus:

There is one simple reason why the last 150 years have been years in which one institution after the other has become autonomous: the task-centered and autonomous institution is the only one that performs. Performance requires clear focus and narrow concentration. Multipurpose institutions do not perform. The achievements of the last 150 years in every single area are achievements of narrow focus, narrow concentration, and parochial self-centered values. All performing institutions of modern society are specialized. All of them are concerned only with their own task. The hospital exists to cure sick people. The fire department exists to prevent and to extinguish fires. The business enterprise exists to satisfy economic wants. The great advances in public health have largely been the result of freestanding organizations that focus on one disease or on one part of the human body and disregard everything else (consider the American Cancer Society, the American Heart Association, the American Lung Society, the American Mental Health Society, and so on).

Whenever an institution goes beyond a narrow focus, it ceases to perform.[7]

Our ability to focus great resources upon individual tasks and products has developed our muscles of achievement. We have mastered industrial productivity, which is increasingly and irreversibly taking place off our shores. But a successful shift from an industrial to a knowledge mindset is a much greater challenge, requiring less reliance on formula, focus, and performance and more on the complementary attributes of imagination, wonder, and risk. The U.S. began this process of adaptation with a false start in the seventies when organizations over-conceived their range of responsibility. Walls were coming down everywhere: in Berlin, in kitchens, and in schoolrooms. Churches became, not only places of worship, but soup kitchens and homeless shelters. Schools became, not only places to learn to read and write, but counseling centers and feeding stations.

Our interior muscles of cohesion simply were not strong enough to perform in such unfocused environments, and the result was inflation at every level, economic and academic. When we lost our balance, we began to panic. Whereas the large muscles of performance are enhanced by fear and crisis, the finer muscles of variety and ambiguity can be short-circuited by urgency. Before we found a new center of gravity for these broader functions, we froze and retreated to familiar industrial ways of management. Dan Yankelovich, in his analysis of the movement of social trends over long periods of time, calls this phenomenon *lurch and learn*. Like a pendulum, society thrusts itself forward in a new direction until the reaction and counter forces pull it back beyond its original starting place. Ultimately the new force gravitates forward towards a new place—a more evolved center.

Today, in every arena, the anxiety of our times is pulling us backward, more lurch and freeze, than lurch and learn. Everywhere we are admonished towards focus and discipline. In business, it's core competencies; in marketing, it's segments and targets; in education, it's assessment and defined cultural cache— deciding what every fourth grader should know and teaching toward that end. There is an increased focus on single indicators for progress, from shareholders' value to end-of-year tests. And the returns are diminishing. Rote, efficient processes led by a management-by-manual mindset approach to new problems with rehearsed solutions. This tired formula is no longer moving us forward for two reasons: First, this is the Age of Ideas, not the age of the machine. Second, the dominant industrial management tool, tying productivity measures to extrinsic motivation, whether the fear of punishment or the carrot of reward, tends to dull innovation and intellectual performance muscles in the long run. It also pales in strength next to the sustainable and renewable forces of intrinsic motivation: curiosity, freedom, acting on hunches, friendship, pride, and passion.

This failure of Skinnerian psychology was identified long before the current proliferation of incentive plans, benchmarks, and assessment criteria; but the exceptional capacity for some forms of growth produced by external, short-term rewards distracted us from this reality. The prospect of a simple solution to the challenge of managing the human aspect of growth production has been too seductive—"What a fascinating thing! Total control of a living organism!" (B.F. Skinner, 1983).[8]

We all know that the human imagination doesn't breed in captivity. Yet even though we know it for ourselves, we have failed to develop better practices. Unable to let go of the idea of performance long enough to grab hold of what we could know about creativity, we've ushered in the the failure of genuine growth, in both education and industry. As educator Alfie Kohn puts it, we'd been had, not by a failure of effort, but by a failure of ideas.

> There is a time to admire the grace and persuasive power of an influential idea, and there is time to fear its hold over us. The time to worry is when the idea is so widely shared that we no longer even notice it, when it is so deeply rooted that it feels to us like plain common sense. At the point when objections are not answered anymore because they are no longer even raised, we are not in control: we do not have the idea; it has us.[9]

The genius of American business is a two-part harmony: power, strength, magnitude, and will on the one hand; beauty, originality, variety, and individualism on the other. America grew up in the spirit of both Horatio Algier and Ralph Waldo Emerson, and it is at our peril that we forget either. In times of crisis our survival instinct tells us to drop baggage, thank goodness. But in the aftermath of crisis, we must guard our center of gravity. As we begin to grow again, we cannot assume that the forces are still in balance.

Business is scared. And in our obsession with belt-tightening and focused performance, our organizations are careening towards unsustainable concepts of growth. In the Age of Ideas, the seed corn will be contradiction, ecotonic disruption, and re-creation for our next generation of growth. The rich soil, however, will be the entrepreneurial vision and ingenuity that served us so well in the Industrial Age.

# 2

# *Discovering Imaginative Intelligence*

*The dogmas of the quiet past are inadequate to the stormy present. The occasion is piled high with difficulty, and we must rise with the occasion. As our case is new, so we must think anew and act anew. We must disenthrall ourselves.*

–Abraham Lincoln

*The real voyage of discovery consists not only in seeking new landscapes but in having new eyes.*

–Marcel Proust

Fat times are over. In an environment where real growth is no longer the norm, the focus of resources in every field must be redirected to the cultivation of fertile and diverse sources of new markets, products, and processes. The next generation of great leaders will come from those who know how to translate as well as direct.

Command and control management is too slow and costly for these times. Traditional strategies, pushing harder in the same direction or a closer counting of beans, will be insufficient for the Age of Ideas. It is a time for smart, supple leaders who learn as they lead, and lead as they learn. Their sources for learning and leading will come from beyond the walls of any one discipline or the constraints of a single approach.

The medieval practice of putting a moat around the castle to protect its integrity from invasion is useless for our times, whether the castle is a company, a department, or a discipline. Leadership for the idea generation will come, not from those who resist or ignore the invasion of complex and contradictory ideas, but from those who recognize new forces and learn to ride them well. The new challenge for organizational integrity is to get better at listening to the conversations at the crossroads, rather than guarding the gates. The creative potential of any organization is its greatest resource.

**Command and control management is too slow and costly for these times**

As we encounter the exhaustible limits of our material environment, success in turbulent, non-linear circumstances will demand radical changes in our assumptions and practices. Real future value will come from the capacity to originate new ideas, organizations, markets, products, and services; and it will be led by innovators. Companies will need to expose and explode formulaic practices, the priorities, processes, structures, and organizational behaviors that have guided them in the past.

In order to innovate, to find new insights and inventive solutions to increasingly complex problems, organizations and individuals must set out on a journey of total transformation into the unknown, acknowledging and embracing experimentation, risk, and failure. This is a journey most are reluctant to take, but must in order to achieve an artesian well of creative innovation.

## *Growth is not an accounting process*

The central tenet of this book is that sustainable growth is a creative process, not an accounting practice. Many of today's businesses are organized for failure. Long-term innovation in the Age of Ideas will require a new understanding of the way companies are structured and take action. Our current understanding of growth through systematic innovation is miserably insufficient for the task; it requires neither a tweak nor an overhaul, but a complete re-imagining.

> **Sustainable growth is a creative process, not an accounting practice.**

Real transformation will require organizations to become creative learning marketplaces, collaborative exchanges at the crossroads, trading on the knowledge, ideas, insights, art, and cultures of multiple disciplines. Technology will be an important tool, but a creative culture will be the foundation. Growing what we have come to call *imaginative intelligence* requires the kind of inventive, flexible thinking, fresh insights, dynamic vision, and expansiveness of perspective that invite connections from multiple sources.

In the Age of Ideas, the greatest asset of an organization is its people. Real leverage against the bottom line will be driven by creative development and utilization of individual and collective imaginations. To prosper in these times, organizations must actively work to supply the nutrients, stimuli, and knowledge that help prepare the collective mind, and to increase their ability to make the unlikely connections that ultimately lead to growth.

The organization of the future must be a place where all of us have the freedom and the challenge to grow our individual imaginative intelligences. Creativity will no longer be considered the elite province of the creative department, a new product team, or the new ventures group. Rather, a business as a whole must be in a natural state of ongoing generativity; a marketplace of exchange for discovering and trading ideas that make a difference; a world where creativity and innovation are a part of the invisible fabric.

The vigorous, creative companies that will prevail in unpredictable times will need leaders that understand how to unleash and liberate potential, not guard privilege and systems—leaders with energy and aptitude for creating new things, doing things differently, sensing what's possible, managing change, and, ultimately, marshalling the resources to make it happen. More than any time before, the Age of Ideas will require leaders with imaginative intelligence.

### Imaginative intelligence

There is no standardized test for imaginative intelligence, but if there were, most of the answers would be *(E) All of the above.*[1] When we tap into our imaginative intelligence, we can hear our inner voice while remaining open to the vastness of new possibilities. We develop richer thought patterns; we learn to convert the raw material of our experiences into inventive work; and we find new ways of getting things done and new portals for seeing what could be done.

> **There is no standardized test for imaginative intelligence.**

For a medical student, it's the difference between getting an *A* in organic chemistry and knowing how to take a patient's history and make a diagnosis; for a teacher it's the difference between knowing the material and knowing how to make it matter to students. It's about seeing how things are and imagining how they could be different. It's about timing and taste, guessing and revising, sensing and saying, dreaming and remembering. It seems easy, occurs often in children, but is difficult to sustain.

Imaginative intelligence is the capacity to originate new ideas and the ability to cultivate them as individuals and as a community. There are two parts to understanding and developing imaginative intelligence. The first is individual and involves each person's capacity to think and work inventively, problem-solve with elasticity, and ideate creatively; to see new possibilities, combinations, and fresh solutions; to envision and develop new patterns in existing fields as well as new fields themselves. It is informed by continuous, diverse sources of interest and knowledge, both specific and broad-based. It is fueled by intrinsic motivation.

The second part is organizational, the imaginative intelligence of the collective entity. It is a function of how the organization is structured and how it acts. Defined largely by culture, information flows, diversity, collective knowledge, and environment, it fuels a company's ability to sustainably create innovative growth.

Both facets of imaginative intelligence are characterized by the ability to imagine, the freedom to discover, access to voice, speed in working in sketch-pad form, the quality of contradiction, understanding of story, skill in conversation, a high level of generosity, and the ability to align the function and feel of space. Exploring each level as well as the links between them has been a major focus of *The Odyssey Project on Imaginative Intelligence*. [See Chapter 3.]

## *Real growth and imaginative intelligence*

Building imaginative intelligence both at the personal and organizational levels is ultimately critical for generating the kind of growth that is sustainable. Top-line growth achieved through the creation of innovative products, processes, and services is the real mark of an innovator. Sustainable growth, generated either internally (*organic growth*) or from truly strategic acquisitions and synergistic mergers, has been the hardest to achieve. The growth never seems to happen, yet is the most promising when given the high-octane fuel of imaginative intelligence.

Organic growth, the growth rate of a company excluding any growth from takeovers, acquisitions, or mergers, is considered the "true growth for the core of a company."[2] This concept was rarely mentioned during the juice-up-the-earnings acquisition and merger mania era. Strategic mergers and acquisitions are appropriate as a complimentary strategy to organic growth, but not as a substitute for it. M&A activity can be an effective way to achieve economies of scale, enter new market and product segments, and expand intellectual capital, among other things. The kind of growth we take issue with is the dominant two-pronged form of growth that CEOs most often fall back on today: growth through massive and obsessive cost cutting, endless belt-tightening that has either strangled or starved off real future growth, and growth through serial acquisitions and consolidations, aggressive accounting practices, and artificial financial engineering. None of these are sustainable.

Warren Buffet writes:

> If you've been a reader of financial reports in recent years, you've seen a flood of "pro-forma" earnings statements—tabulations in which managers invariably show "earnings" far in excess of those allowed by their auditors. In these presentations, the CEO tells his owners "don't count this, don't count that—just count what makes earnings fat." Often, a forget-all-this-bad-stuff message is delivered year after year without management so much as blushing.[3]

Ironically, my first in-depth experience with the power and the pleasure of creating organic growth came while I was working for the Interpublic Group of Companies (IPG), a company that bought 185 companies between 1999 and 2001.[4] As a newly minted CEO and Chairman of Long Haymes Carr, I had been with Madison Avenue megafirm, Ammirati Puris Lintas, a firm *that* which had virtually doubled in size overnight through the merger of Ammirati & Puris and Lintas Advertising. When I got the call from the CEO about taking on a new opportunity, I was hoping for Singapore. They gave me North Carolina.

The mission was not exotic or easy. They wanted more top line growth and bottom line profits—fast. Without the luxury of time to let new programs unfold gradually, everything had to be jacked up simultaneously. Systems, people, clients, pitches, planning, recruiting, training, alliances, compensation, facilities, and technology. I would need the whole force of my imagination to create the business, energy, connections, fast breaks, and night-before-the-pitch perseverance it takes to turn an ad company around.

I accepted the challenge. I'd had success over time creating growth for other firms—Procter & Gamble, Sara Lee, Unilever—and now I had my own canvas. Over the next six years, I pulled together a team of smart, diverse, inventive people and together we delivered. Long Haymes Carr was a competitive, successful, innovative force. We had a phenomenal run.[5]

In short order, we won twelve out of twelve new business competitions and *Adweek* magazine named us Southeastern Agency of the Year. We grew the agency from the hundredth largest to the fiftieth largest U.S. advertising agency and set our sites on the national stage.[6] We developed pioneering programs to encourage organization-wide innovation—Creative Odyssey, LHC University, and Digital Storytelling—earning national recognition and attention from *Fast Company, BusinessWeek,* and *Time.*[7] By Christmas of 2000, these programs were in full flight and the agency had cultivated a fantastic roster of clients with which to grow, including Champion, Hanes, Journeys, Sealy, Thomasville, Wachovia, and Virgin[8]. In the fourth quarter of that year alone, we won millions in new business in competitive shootouts including Alabama Power, Dunlop/Maxfli/Slazenger, Midway Airlines and T.J. Maxx.[9]

The free market is the ultimate arbiter of real value over time. In a six-year period, we grew from a dependency on a North Carolina clientele into a super-regional with clients from Boston to Dallas.

Through our instincts, experiments, and willingness to take risks, we evolved a business model focused on three components of creative growth: (1) building up core expertise in each discipline, (2) inventing new ways to build imaginative thinking and creative problem solving skills, and (3) recognizing and leveraging the unique talents and passions of our people. As we developed strength in each area, we also nurtured a dynamic culture of creativity and innovation that flowed through all areas, resulting in a powerful magic.

Nonetheless, the process required an ongoing recommitment to creativity as a counterforce to mediocrity. We intended to achieve success by design, not drift. Harvard professor Teresa M. Amabile observes,

> When I consider all the organizations I have studied and worked with over the past 22 years, there can be no doubt: creativity gets killed much more often than it gets supported. For the most part, this isn't because managers have a vendetta against creativity. On the contrary, most believe in the value of new and useful ideas. However, creativity is undermined unintentionally every day in the work environments that were established—for entirely good reasons—to maximize business imperatives such as coordination, productivity, and control.[10]

At LHC, we discovered that it is possible for business imperatives and creativity to flourish together. In fact, when they are effectively linked, they fuel each other. We invented as we went along.

### Building the agency

- **Inventive problem solving skills:** We developed the *Creative Odyssey,* an ongoing, systematic immersion in the leading edge elements of the pop culture.[11]
- **Learning to think and communicate in real time:** We had George Stephanopoulous come to the agency to talk with us about his experience putting together the famous 24/7 communications War Room for the first Clinton presidential election.[12]
- **Presentation skills:** We bypassed the traditional, canned packages available and went to the prestigious faculty at the North Carolina School of the Arts to study theater, drama, and ensemble techniques.
- **Building expertise:** We developed LHC University, a dynamic training program designed to bring the brightest minds from a diverse array of fields to the agency for lectures, workshops, and projects.
- **Expanding intellectual capital:** We created numerous strategic alliances with the best practitioners to work with our people and our clients on projects. This approach allowed us to add significant value and tap otherwise impossible-to-reach talent while controlling costs.
- **Designing a new kind of workspace:** We brought celebrated installation artist Stephen Hendee in to transform a highly trafficked, sterile conference room into a space *Fast Company* called "a cave-like den of inspiration."[13]
- **Increasing productivity:** We battled the stress and long hours inherent in advertising agency life by offering on-site classes in tai chi, meditation, and yoga. We brought in professional masseuses, nutritionists, and feng-shui practitioners to support an over-extended work force, and immediately sensed improvement in the quality of our work.[14]

Our focus on growing organically at LHC necessitated that we find new ways to unleash latent talent and build imaginative intelligence in a systematic and sustained way. Our programs were designed to develop mental agility for the discovery of new angles and strategies, and the capacity to see how experience and naiveté, intuition and reason, spontaneous and planned actions, creativity and practicality, passion and logic could all be used to create growth and new value.

**We discovered that it was possible for business imperatives and creativity to flourish together.**

My six years at LHC whetted my appetite to know more. Having tasted the pleasure and power of real organic growth, I was a horse out of the barn.

## The search

Where to? I had a hunch the real news for business wasn't going to be found in business. I had been running with the big boys long enough to know they were running on empty. At LHC our greatest breakthroughs were being fueled by ideas that came primarily from insights across non-business disciplines of knowledge: psychology, science, politics, poetry, music, art, architecture, religion, philosophy. These are voices largely unheeded in the business world. I wondered if there was a way to reinvision business toward the possibility of such a confluence of diverse thinking and experience.

That was the beginning of this journey, the search to find those folks who see things differently—the mad dogs, dreamers, and sages; the search to find original sources of real growth, creativity, and innovation and to get beyond the clichés, platitudes, and the superficial surface; to draw on the uncommon wisdom and insights of leaders across multiple disciplines as we search for novel approaches, new attitudes, different viewpoints, and fresh perspectives.

## Launching the expedition

I joined forces with my friend Jane Stephens, and we set out to identify examples and patterns of imaginative growth. One of the first people we approached for ideas was Phil Hanes. We asked him where he would start.

"That's easy," he said. "T George Harris is the smartest guy I know. You've got to get to California—you'll know where to go from there."

Hanes was right. The connections unfolded as I went—from Harris, the maverick editor of *Psychology Today,* to the Sundance Institute in Utah; from the Guinness factory in Ireland to the open source guru at Stanford; from IDEO, the human behavior group that invented the mouse to Dan Yankelovich who re-invented public opinion polling and dialogue strategies. From poet Maya Angelou, who revitalized the power of storytelling, to architects Denise Scott Brown and Robert Venturi, who reconceived the function and aesthetic of public buildings. And on and on—we sought out artists and thinkers who were exploring the edges of their own universes.

## What does it look like?

Imaginative intelligence looks different in every situation, but the commonalities are as palpable as the differences.

It might look like *Psychology Today* under the tenure of T George Harris. When he took over the fledgling magazine as editor-in-chief in 1967, Harris had already tested his power for tapping into America's thinking as a reporter for *Time, Life,* and *Fortune;* but he had a hunch that American readers were ready for something different.

You may remember the newsstands in those days—*Time, Newsweek, Life,* and *Look* shared space with the comic books, from *Archie* to *Superman;* the women's magazines, from *Good Housekeeping* to *Redbook;* then there was *National Geographic, Popular Mechanics, TV Guide,* and *Playboy.* That was it. If you wanted to read about ideas and developments in a field of learning, you had to go to the library.

Harris believed that everyday Americans had a rich curiosity, a desire to learn for the sake of learning, especially about their own abilities and interests. In order to develop *Psychology Today,* he couldn't simply borrow readers from other social science journals or *Archie* or *Playboy;* he had to invent a new readership, a whole new phenomenon of public reading. Nor was he able to borrow from an available cadre of academic researchers and psychologists. Other than professionals in the field, who would subscribe to a journal with more footnotes than writing, more method than discovery?

Harris used *Psychology Today* to define a body of knowledge, conversation, and research that had never existed before. People like B. F. Skinner, Rollo May, and Margaret Meade shared data and insights with him about people—how they thought, acted, and believed. What they found at *Psychology Today* was more than a publication. It was a network of idea-makers, research, friendships, conversations, and careers; it was the beginning of a journalism of social studies. Whole conceptual areas were born out of the work and fun of Harris's office, home, and virtual roundtable as one spilled in and out of another.

Or imaginative intelligence might look like Willow Creek Community Church in the suburbs of Chicago. As a twenty-four year old youth leader, Bill Hybels had a vision for building a church. From the beginning he eschewed the cut-the-pie-smaller and take-more-pieces approach. He knew enough about the traditional churches in the area to see that there were still plenty of empty pews available on Sunday mornings, and that no long-term growth for Christianity would be gained by siphoning off worshippers from one church to another. Together with a group of teenagers and leaders from his youth group, Hybels decided to build a church based completely on conversion-growth, filling the pews with people who were not already churchgoers.

Hybels and his group went door to door selling tomatoes from his father's Michigan produce company. As they sold tomatoes, they asked people if they went to church. If people didn't attend a church, Hybel's group would ask them why and record their answers—*boring, irrelevant, unfamiliar, made you feel guilty, embarrassing situations, depressing music, always asking for money, hypocritical, etc.* He would ask, "If we started a church that was different than all that, would you come?"

In September of 1971, Willow Creek Community Church held its first service in a movie theater with forty people. Today it hosts 28,000 worshippers on a forty-acre campus and leads a network of affiliated churches worldwide, reaching millions of individuals on a weekly basis. As he built Willow Creek from conversion-growth in an era when traditional churches are shrinking at exponential rates, Hybels has kept his promise to his tomato customers—the church continues to be different.

In a writer, however, imaginative intelligence might look like Maya Angelou. Poet. Dancer. Political leader. Actress. Playwright. Director. Philanthropist. Educator. Maya Angelou is all of these, but she is also something distinct from any of them. In 1968, before anyone dreamed a black woman would write a book that would be a national bestseller, or that any contemporary bestseller might become required reading for the College Board Advanced Placement exams, Maya Angelou began writing *I Know Why the Caged Bird Sings*. It wasn't fiction or poetry, nor was it religious testimony or the narrative of heroic achievement. It was life as Maya Angelou saw it, heard it, and knew it as a black girl growing up in a changing world.

None of these accomplishments sound radical to us now—a magazine for thoughtful readers, a church for the *irreligious,* the published thoughts of a black woman—but when Harris, Hybels, and Angelou began their work, these ideas were revolutionary. They cleared new space for new worlds, and the host of focus-driven publications, contemporary churches, and autobiographic writing that has followed them has changed the world.

## *Widening the net*

We can borrow from the break-through discoveries these innovators have made within their various fields, but more importantly, we study them in order to adopt a new habit of mind. The journals of Thomas Edison have recently become available—3,500 journals containing four million pages of notes to himself and his colleagues chronicling his observations, experiments, and discoveries. These notebooks reveal a different picture from the one often painted for schoolchildren, the *Every time he failed at making a light bulb he learned one more way not to do it* lesson. That makes him sound boring, like a machine that just systematically worked through the universe until it finally discovered the light bulb.

But what these journals reveal is not a highly ordered, product-driven, systematic thinker, but a dreamer, a wanderer, and a wonderer. His notes include everything from ideas for designing an airplane (generations before the Wright brothers), to poetry about his neighbors' habits, to the smell of a bug outside his office. (This tidbit intrigued him so much that he wrote a letter to Darwin about it.) Edison's notes to himself show a capacity not so much for dogged perseverance, but for extraordinarily rich ongoing conversation with himself— conversation that is tentative, exploratory, loose, imaginative, and ultimately productive.

This has been the goal of my journey this year, to make new connections, to see unlikely juxtapositions, and ultimately to discover nourishing sustenance for original thought and action. I wanted to expand my inner intellectual geography, and I wanted to take it with me as I returned to business.

How did Edison sustain this rich inner dialogue while at the same time effecting such productivity? With a sense of democracy uncommon in nineteenth-century organizations, Edison was able to infect every person in his lab with the capacity for connected thinking and imaginative leaps.

As the other scientists, as well as the janitors, began to record their reflections and ideas, the resulting breadth of discovery was unparalleled by any scientific team. Edison himself applied for over one thousand patents during his lifetime, and with his encouragement, Edison's associates at every level of his shop applied for patents in their own names. Both the dialogue and the productivity were contagious, and they made for good business.

As we develop our imaginative intelligence, we allow ourselves to pull inspiration from a wide range of sources, to trust the creative process, and to draw on the innovator within all of us. Ultimately, as change becomes the status quo, creativity becomes an essential and indivisible part of the enjoyment of everyday work. We learn to direct and enjoy the ride, rather than being thrown by it. We become like boiling water; even cold water poured on us will heat up and transform.

## 3
## The Odyssey Project
## On Imaginative Intelligence

*Man's mind stretched to a new idea never goes
back to its original dimensions.*

–Oliver Wendell Holmes

*It is difficult
to get the news from poems
yet men die miserably every day
for lack
of what is found there.*

–William Carlos Williams

How does imaginative intelligence manifest itself? Sometimes quite dramatically, like in Jan Demczur, the World Trade Center window washer who freed five Wall Street executives and himself from a disabled elevator during the September 11 disaster. This Ukrainian immigrant used his squeegee handle to pry the door open and the blade to cut a 12-inch hole through three layers of dry wall. As the six of them climbed out of the dark elevator and into the men's room on the 50th floor, surely all of the executives recognized the imaginative intelligence of the maintenance worker.

But what does it look like in a sustained situation? How does an individual or organization develop the capacity to discover resources and generate genuine innovation in ongoing ways? How do we keep our collective imaginations cooking on high for the long haul? We began *The Odyssey Project on Imaginative Intelligence* because we wanted to capture the process of discovery in its primal form—at the transformational boiling point, when liquid gives way to steam, when a hunch grows into an idea.

With our tendency to caricaturize history, many of us have come to envision great breakthrough discoveries as a series of explosive announcements—Columbus returning to Spain with a new map of the world or Copernicus looking up from his calculations and pronouncing that the earth was not the center of the universe.

These "Copernican moments" were, of course, not isolated moments. In fact, they were not moments at all, but axial lifetimes spent sputtering toward discovery, and their sputtering was challenged, fueled, and carried along by the multiple forces at play in the times and contexts from which they grew. Nonetheless, there are, in every field and for every era, individuals who seem to ride the tide farther and shape the thinking of their times in a more pronounced or discernible way.

Imagine, for instance, the economic and intellectual world of Europe five hundred years ago. With the Spanish conquest of the Moors in 1492, the entire landmass had been carved into distinct empires and the scope of the world was defined. The world leaders were competing for stock in a limited venture. Then two guys changed it up: Christopher Columbus, a gold-seeking ship captain whose random misfire on finding a quick route to the Far East landed him on American soil and Nicolaus Copernicus, a Polish priest, who recalculated the center of the universe. Were the dramatic changes wrought by their discoveries the result of imaginative intelligence?

Anyone who could cross the Atlantic Ocean in a boat made from wood and a sail made before the invention of nylon must have had both imagination and intelligence. But, in a sense, the janitor in the World Trade Center with the squeegee had something different than Columbus's raw courage and resourceful ambition—he not only found a way out of the elevator, but he also took the other five guys with him. Columbus, on the other hand, ended up alone. The diary of his final American voyage reads like a near cartoon of desertion and one-up-manship in a desperate effort to get home first with the gold. Columbus himself died broke, never knowing he'd discovered a new world, leaving a horrific legacy of terror in the wake of the Spanish conquest of America.[1]

What about Copernicus? A more scholarly man than Columbus, Copernicus spent his life working on a world-shaking theory that the dominion of Earth is not the central force in the universe. Despite the limitations of primitive instruments and the incessantly cloudy weather of his little Polish town, Copernicus completely reconceived the scope of the universe from the derivations of countless, carefully measured calibrations of the sky. Yet he, too, could have failed to take the world with him.

In the last years of Copernicus's life, a young man named George Rheticus moved into his home and persuaded him to publish his work. As the story goes, Nicolaus Copernicus died as he finally read the printed title page of the first printed copy of his *Celestial Orbs*, his "hypothesis" that became the touchstone for Galileo, Newton, and Einstein.

Forgotten by history, George Rheticus was an *expediter,* a term we borrow from the restaurant business. The expediter holds the flex position on the wait staff of cutting-edge restaurants. They are the extra hands, the generalists who keep the orders moving and make sure everything gets to the table.

Convinced that many of the great breakthroughs of our own times are delivered too reluctantly through the self-preserving systems of traditional disciplines and across the barriers that divide them, we began to design a systematic study of the Copernican forces of different spheres of understanding in today's world. In a sense, we conceived *The Odyssey Project* in the spirit of the expediter—getting the good stuff out of the kitchen and on the table.

One Friday morning early in the project, we were bent over our notes and stacks of books in our corner of a coffee shop, when a friend walked by, saying, "Don't get up. I'll come back later. I don't want to take you away from your madmen and dreamers." The name stuck. Some of our madmen were women, and some of them were more sage than mad, so we expanded the idea a bit. But in a very real way they had become ours, and our meetings with them became the foundational work for this book.

## The methodology

We ultimately focused our research work on ground-breaking individuals in fifteen different fields: advertising, architecture, art, communications, composition, design, film-making, future studies, journalism, poetry, psychology, public opinion analysis, religion, scriptwriting, and theatre. Each field has its own history, vocabulary, and benchmarks for achievement, so the criteria through which we identified our mad dogs were necessarily and intentionally broad. *We were looking for individuals who demonstrated imaginative intelligence in its fullest sense. People who had the capacity to originate new ideas, to translate their ideas across multiple platforms and disciplines, to develop and sustain rich, ongoing environments for new growth, and who had a history of ongoing re-invention over time, despite cycles of growth and decline in their fields and in the larger economy.*

Through our research we wanted to identify Copernican leaders of our day and study the qualities that have rendered them able to imagine a world different than others in their field or times—and bring it to pass. We interviewed, listened to, and studied countless innovators during our two years of study and, in a real sense, all of them show up in the pages of this book, but some of them come into closer view. (For a description of our "mad dogs" and the reasons we chose them for the study, see Part III).

## The mad dogs, dreamers and sages:

- **Maya Angelou,** poet, author, and civic leader
- **Ralph Ardill,** director at Imagination
- **Nancy Beach,** director of programming at Willow Creek Community Church
- **Denise Scott Brown & Robert Venturi,** architects
- **Fu-Ding Cheng,** filmmaker, artist, shaman
- **Joan Darling,** actress, director, producer, and writer
- **Peter Elbow,** professor of English, University of Massachusetts
- **Carol Gilligan,** professor of psychology, Harvard University
- **Chris Hardman,** founder of Antennae Audio and Antenna Theatre
- **T George Harris,** journalist and former editor-in-chief of *Psychology Today*
- **Joe McCarthy,** CEO of McCarthy Mambro Bertino Advertising
- **Robert Redford,** actor, director, producer, and founder of Sundance Institute
- **Jane Fulton Suri,** director of human factors design & research at IDEO
- **Richard Tate and Whit Alexander,** founders of Cranium Inc.
- **Alvin Toffler,** author and futurist
- **Kirk Varnedoe,** art historian, Princeton's Institute of Advanced Studies
- **Daniel Yankelovich,** social scientist and founder of the Yankelovich Monitor

And, of course, our ideas and discoveries also come from our own experiences of twenty years of exploration and discovery in our respective fields of business and education. From the world of Procter & Gamble to the big show on Madison Avenue, from our work with top Fortune 500 companies to entrepreneurial start-ups, from Kenyan schoolrooms to large universities, we've had a chance to see countless mad dogs, dreamers, and sages at work.

## What did we find?

What we found were individuals whose awareness of their fields and ability to imagine them differently had given them an extraordinarily elastic capacity for making things happen. What we found were new ways of discovering—and discarding—rules. The process and products of imaginative intelligence looked different in every arena and for every individual, but the commonalities were as palpable as the differences.

### Some of the personal attributes our subjects had in common:

- High-amperage personalities with a white-hot passion for their work. Working consciously to keep their fires lit, they lead from a fire in the belly. Their energy is contagious—you feel the lift when you are with them.
- A visceral and practical understanding of the serious creative process that makes improvisation and leaps of imagination possible. Countless hours of intense engagement with the primary material and complex theories. Each has cultivated the well-prepared mind it takes to recognize patterns and see new possibilities.
- A deep respect for the voice of each individual in their environment and a keen awareness of who is not yet at the table.
- An intellectual curiosity and cultivated space for wondering far beyond their field—Varnedoe with math and science, Venturi and Scott Brown with business and commercial vernacular, Redford with the environment. They've learned effective ways to import knowledge from other disciplines.
- A vast and active network of colleagues and friends across diverse fields, a roundtable of kindred spirits.
- With immense adaptivity to change and a capacity for reformulation, they live the question, not the answer.

> **. . . Continued from page 38**
>
> - Humility. Disarmingly unself-protective, they seem relatively unlimited by the blinders of ego.
> - An abiding youthfulness. Childlike in their capacity for wonder, flexibility, enthusiasm, and growth.
> - A talent for seeing problems as opportunities, oddities as resources, and differences as portals, they had a stunning ability to make things happen.
> - A pervasive force on the environment in which they worked and an ability to bring a heightened sense of purpose to it.

## Language matters

More striking than this list of personal qualities, however, we found that these imaginative leaders work out of a unique set of values, a different currency of thinking that tends to generate, rather than limit, connections. They don't only think about different concepts, they think *differently* about different concepts. They speak and think in a different language.

> **"Bad terminology is the enemy of good thinking."**

This is the Age of Ideas. To access its riches we need new tools of invention, arrangement, interpretation, and exchange. These are fundamentally language-based, not number-based or even sequence-based, processes. For the most part, we think in words; and as the complexity of our work becomes greater, we must develop a new vocabulary for conceiving the expanded terrain of business.

As Warren Buffet puts it, "Bad terminology is the enemy of good thinking. When companies or investment professionals use terms such as "EBITDA" and "pro forma," they want you to unthinkingly accept concepts that are dangerously flawed."[2] When we default to clichès, rules of thumb, and business-ease, we not only sound tedious, we make ourselves dangerously vulnerable.

Language is a tenacious governor, and if we are not careful to reformulate the terms and metaphors we use in ongoing ways, our thinking will be hamstrung by the limits of our words. The current business vernacular built on industrial and military images is inadequate for the task. Like playing tennis with a ping pong paddle, the shallowness of our language, our primary instrument for thinking, is unsuited to the scope of our tasks.

To move effectively across environments and access new sources, we need to change the way we think and talk about growth. As T. S. Eliot put it, "We measure out our lives in coffee spoons." Nothing effects our capacity to expand our capacity for understanding as much as language. We need to trade in our coffee spoons. In order to understand business in bigger and more vital ways, we need to move away from its traditional vocabulary; we need to learn to think—and even to dream—about our work in a different language.

To that end, we offer a new palette of tools for genuine growth in the Age of Ideas.

## A New Lexicon – Tools for Developing Imaginative Intelligence

**Discovery:** The process of finding new insight, knowledge, and invention. Discovery requires risk, experimentation, mistakes, and failure. Dead-ends and messy explorations often spawn our greatest successes.

**Story:** The vessel for values, identity, purpose, and personality. Story is a rich resource providing a wealth of identity, powerful kinds of knowing, and insightful understanding. Knowing and communicating who you are—your people and your genius.

**Conversation:** The genuine interactions for listening, changing, growing, and bringing a fuller range of vision to your own expertise. In its root sense, conversation is turning together.

**Contradiction:** The unlikely connections of knowledge provide portals for breakthroughs. Those who learn to read them, mine them, honor them become large and contain multitudes without being relentless or unadaptive, gaining scope without losing personality.

**Voice:** An artesian well, voice is the best resource of each person. It is the most genuine, vital expression and energy which fuel the organization's best work.

**Sketchpad:** Sketchpad is a dynamic for learning and leading on the move, providing ways of getting at possibility, form, and direction, quickly and broadly, without losing momentum.

**Space:** A nourishing environment. A source of stimulation, inspiration, communication. An expression of ethos. Space is a bridge to facilitate flows of information and insight through *siloed* fortifications. A place to capture the full scope of our knowledge.

## Generosity the multiplier

We believe there is a fundamental force at play that expands the power of the individual tools. It is generosity—the multiplier. It is the unaccountable power of the inspiring influence of certain gestures and responses by leaders at the right time. Generosity releases a dynamic energy exchange. Its power is ancient, but its force is contemporary. Beyond any shrewd tactics or stockpile of materials, it has the capacity to stretch our world.

Consider this letter from Nelson Mandela, written a short time after he was released from prison:

> It is not a nice feeling for a man to see his family struggling without security, without the dignity of the head of the family around, but despite the hard times that were had in prisons . . . there have been men who are very good in the sense that they understand our point of view, and they do everything to make you as happy as possible. That has wiped out any bitterness which a man could have.[3]

How does a man spend twenty-seven years in a South African prison as No. 4888/64 and walk out thinking this way? Surely, neither the Afrikaner wardens nor the stream of prisoners he lived with—some political, some homicidal; all beaten, underfed, and angry—would have encouraged Mandela to see the bright side of human nature day in and day out. But from the accounts of guards as well as fellow prisoners, Mandela made a conscious decision to alter the vicious environments of racism and prisons.

From the first days of his long imprisonment, Mandela told fellow prisoners the sober truth as he saw it, "Look, you chaps shouldn't have any illusions about how long you are going to be here. In all probability you are going to sit out the entire period." Then he would push them to look beyond the hatred and the staggering limitations surrounding them to see the possibilities beyond. "Let's spend some time strategizing. Let's see how we can transform the situation on the island."[4] With a generosity that was habitual and studied, instinctive and shrewd, Mandela re-structured the moral economy of his prison life and ultimately of his whole country.

There is unaccountable power in the inspiring influence of certain gestures and responses by *big people* at the right time. Generosity is not drawn from an expense account, but from a leader's sense of humility, humanity, and timing. Particularly when the wells have run dry, when the patience and imagination of everyone else has worn thin, the open-handed generosity of a wise leader can jump start a new generation of growth. As mind-stretchers, terrain-claimers, and word-givers, leaders can reset the prime rate of exchange between the members of their working communities.

> **There is unaccountable power in the inspiring influence of certain gestures and responses by *big people* at the right time.**

More than ever, we need leaders to be the grown-ups for our communities. Philosopher Cornel West points out that in times following periods of dramatic change—after the Welfare Act of Charles Dickens's England, after the Civil War in the U.S., and now after the Civil Rights legislation of the seventies—there has been a tendency to freeze backward, regressing toward simplistic thinking and reactive behaviors. As West puts it, "The new idea is born, but not grown-up. We've become ossified in a state of adolescence."[5]

There is a myth in our culture that hard times make people grow up fast, but it's not necessarily true. Often hard times, whether the throes of family conflict or the pressures of financial recession, have the opposite effect. They make us shrink, lay low, and run for cover. Working or living in a shrinking environment leaves us with a sense of scarcity and desperation that is hard to shake, even when the situation is alleviated.

The myth persists, however, because, against a backdrop of scarcity and harshness, our models of strength and kindness stand taller. We see them more clearly and are marked by them more definitely. There's nothing good about living in a prison, going to bed hungry, or working at a job that doesn't work. Hard times and scant resources, unmitigated by the presence of someone like Mandela, ultimately limit growth and diminish the human spirit. Nonetheless, in all times, and even more so in hard times, the generous actions and words of a magnanimous leader can make an immeasurable difference. They help us to grow up despite hard times. They transform the economy of scarcity, blame-laying, and turf-grabbing into one of abundance. The resources don't change, but we do. And, because it is hard won, it can be a change that endures.

In the era of ideas, we have unprecedented possibilities for growth for all people. Whereas the economies of agriculture and industry were based on a scarcity model, and in many cases worked better when the imagery of scarcity and competitive forces were invoked, the idea era is much less driven by the profit-loss seesaw. Your good ideas don't necessarily take away from mine, nor are they diminished when you share them with me. This may be a concept our generation will never fully be able to accept.

As we deal with the challenge of recalibrating systems of ownership and exchange in the Age of Ideas, those who have been schooled in the art of generosity will continue to have a great advantage. They will have a foundational sense of the possibility of a non-diminishing exchange of energy and knowledge. They will be well-suited to work in communities built on fluid exchange and collaboration. They will believe that their workplaces can both draw from them and give to them at the same time. They will insist on environments that foster generativity over depletion, freedom over restraint, expansion over limits, and gratitude over entitlement.

The dreamers and sages we studied have an extraordinary sense of generosity about themselves and their insights, and an uncanny ability to give themselves away through language. They are disarmingly unself-protective, but speak with a sense of heightened awareness about both the fun and the seriousness of their work. They are big people, who have stretched the members and the concepts of their respective disciplines. They have demanded that the rules of the game be made more expansive and hospitable to a broader world in need of genuine growth.

By bringing together leaders from discreet fields of learning, we are extending the ethos of their generosity. Putting an ear to the walls that separate them, we've listened hard through different worlds of language, methodology, values, and histories. We've done so in hope of kindling a new exchange of meaning and of furthering our mutual work of developing replenishable and ongoing sources of growth.

# A New Lexicon for the Age of Ideas

Part II

# 4

# *Discovery*

*Come to the edge.*
*It's too high.*
*Come to the edge!*
*We might fall.*
*COME TO THE EDGE!!*
*So they came, and he pushed them…*
*And they flew.*

—Guillaume Apollinaire

Ideas are the manifestations of discovery, the process of finding new insight, knowledge, and innovation. In the organization, as in nature, discovery is an inherently messy process that involves risk, experimentation, mistakes, dead-ends, and failures. In creative companies the leadership team must create a fertile environment where discovery happens, not just in moments of crisis, but every day, not just in the periphery, but in the core. This risky exploration is necessary to successful innovation and sustainable growth.

Companies do not *intentionally* kill innovation, but let it die before the game even starts. They are unwilling to pay the price of admission. Risk is the entry fee for real growth. There are companies that pay lip service to risk-taking, but are intolerant of the failures and mistakes that come with it; and their employees know it. Successful businesses of the Industrial Age valued efficiency, productivity, and control. Today these very hallmarks of strength erode and undermine the process of discovery and growth through innovation.

There is a better way. Productivity and innovation are both driven by discovery, the ongoing process of seeing more each day in the people, systems, service, products, exchanges, and culture of a business. To uncover the great resources of their companies, leaders must change their thinking about the creative process itself and learn to access the intrinsic motivational drives that fuel discovery.

### The miner's lamp

The process of innovation is the long, sweaty work of digging through tons of information for a few golden nuggets to put together in a new combination, a fresh idea. "Innovators make unlikely new knowledge combinations from diverse isolated, often contradictory, knowledge silos," says T George Harris. At Harris's home in La Jolla, California, the object lesson hangs just to the left of the front door. It is an old leather mule yoke. The most coveted award of achievement at *Psychology Today* during Harris's tenure, the weather-beaten yoke is a symbol of the hard work of discovery, the plowing that prepares the ground for new ideas to flourish.

> **Innovation is an activity open to everyone, not just the creative elite.**

Harris points to the yoke and invokes Drucker, his long-time friend and mentor, "Peter would say innovation is not a gift, it's an activity—more perspiration than inspiration."

Innovation is an activity open to everyone, not just the *creative elite* in a thunderbolt of inspiration. Quite the contrary, it is the daily work of what Harris calls the *everyday innovator* to tap the latent creativity inside each of us. "A more useful model of innovation would be the miner's headlamp than the *Eureka* flash.

Intuition is pattern recognition by minds saturated with appropriate information."

Weaving this concept of the miner's lamp into an organization's fabric is the first step in reversing the limitations of the 80/20 rule. From our own experience, we have seen the liberating effect, the jet stream of energy and ideas released in an organization when management shifts its mindset away from the star player mentality and begins to challenge each player to play for keeps.

## A team sport

Basketball coach Pat Riley put it well, "The team on the floor is the team of the moment." Management has the responsibility to coach the team on the floor to the best of its ability and to stop the *if only we had better people* excuses. Leaders need to focus on developing the best in the people they have, while continuously searching for new people to augment that talent.

Kirk Varnedoe, formerly the Chief Curator of Painting and Sculpture for New York's Museum of Modern Art (MOMA), adds another layer to our understanding of innovation through discovery. He says discovery requires more than one discoverer— we need those who create the breakthroughs and those who recognize the breakthroughs. "It's all sterile, unless somebody agrees it's a great idea."

Varnedoe is a master of discovery with a keen eye for transformational moments and the movement of new ideas into society. His pivotal MOMA retrospectives of Sy Twombly, Jasper Johns, and Jackson Pollock have broadened our thinking and shown us what can be gained from innovation.

On a rainy summer day in the 1970s, Varnedoe made a pilgrimage to the north of England to a playing field at the Rugby School. He tells us about the plaque on the wall next to the field that reads:

*This stone commemorates the exploits of William Webb Ellis, who with a fine disregard for the rules of football as played in his time, first took the ball in his arms and ran with it, thus originating the distinctive feature of the Rugby game. A.D. 1823.*

Varnadoe comments,

The thing that always fascinates me is why didn't they throw him out of the game? It's a game with rules, and the guy violated the rules. Let's give credit to the people on the sidelines, who said, 'That's useful, that's not a default, that's not a defect, that's potentially an addition. That's something new; that's not just a violation of the rules, that's the suggestion of a new way of playing.' And so it's the dialogue between his instinct to do it and their instinct to see that it's useful. That's the symbiosis between the structure that a society has and its receptivity to innovation.

This charmed moment of fertilization of a gesture, a thought, or an idea that might otherwise have gone barren is the ground on which organizational leaders must build their knowledge enterprises.

## The looser the chain, the stronger the bond

Innovation must evolve out of the process of individual and collective discovery. Companies cannot command, dictate or force it. If organizations insist on total control, they will remain the same. They must be willing to throw out the traditions, conventions, and orthodoxies that limit experimentation and the flow of new ideas.

Discovery requires new blood and new energy, which only retain their vitality if intrinsically driven from within the passions and interests of the individuals. Once a new idea with potential surfaces, the organization must act with speed to crystallize and mobilize a community of people and resources around it. Centralized command and control management is usually too slow and too removed from the energy of the opportunity.

The company has to be committed to receive and support new ideas, to resource and nurture invention, to harness the speed and momentum inherent in the discovery process and see where in the marketplace the innovative jujitsu move can be made.

## Charles Darwin, not Henry Ford

The metaphor of evolutionary biology is a better business model for the Age of Ideas than is the precision production of the Industrial Age. Many large organizations today, however, still focus on perfecting industrial techniques with computer-driven productivity, off-shore production, just-in-time raw material and inventory controls—the list goes on. That's fine for efficiency, but not for real growth.

The problem for would-be innovators is that these short-term substitutes have become the dominant management models and mindsets. Our obsession with rote, lock-step efficiency has become an ideological albatross, a self-fulfilling prophecy of diminishing returns for cultivating the development of people and ideas, the source of innovation.

The process of discovery, like evolutionary biology, is unpredictable and disorderly, but by the nature of its freedom it spawns the incredibly rich variety which enables its survival. Meanwhile, it considers the unnecessary—the peculiar, the mutant, and the redundant—not as waste products, but as byproducts, valuable raw material for future study.

## Know what you don't know

Embodied in the process of discovery is the idea that we need to know what we don't know. Thrusting ourselves into the unknown is how we experience the source material of new ideas, how we expand and learn. The challenge for the organization is to find ways to build a discovery process into the heart of the company rather than relegating it to the periphery of skunk works and off-sites. In the past we've been advised to play it safe–*Don't ask a question you don't know the answer to*–but for new opportunities to emerge we must ask the questions that we can't yet answer. Embracing the unknown, instead of avoiding it, is a frightening prospect for most organizations. The unpredictability and inefficient nature of discovery make us long for a tidier way. The reality of discovery is akin to Churchill's assessment of the democratic form of government: "Democracy is the worst form of government except for all the others."

**We need to know what we don't know.**

As exhausting as it is to take risks and to wrestle with chaos every day, discovery ultimately leads to ongoing renewal, refreshing its players and its systems with ongoing intrinsic value; whereas the slow burn of old systems ultimately consume them. If we neglect to challenge our people, we not only drain our physical resources, but we drain our human resources, setting them up for the burnout that Peter Drucker warns against:

> We have put too much emphasis on promotion and have not challenged people. But, look, it can be done. Let me give you an example. I know a young man, 25, about to become first trumpeter in a major symphony orchestra. He is not going to be a conductor, not going to be first violinist. And nothing makes him happier than the idea of playing

the trumpet for the next 50 years. What does the symphony orchestra do to satisfy people who will never get promoted that General Motors does not do for its engineers or its other professionals?

And it's not just business. I've been around academe for a long time and only a small minority of the really good people don't get tired of it. At age 43, the rest retire on the job, go into mid-life crisis, and either take to the bottle, have a torrid affair with a 19-year-old, or go into psychoanalysis. Of the three cures, psychoanalysis costs the most and takes the longest; otherwise, the results are pretty much the same. And yet there is that small minority who have inner resources, who still keep on. Many of the others wanted to, but the university system wouldn't allow them to; they had to become overspecialized. We have come to organize knowledge work very much on the model of industrial mass production.[1]

## Discovery at work

At LHC we called our model for the discovery process *The Creative Odyssey;* it lived at the core of our culture and drove our business. It included a series of magical mystery tours to New York, London, San Francisco, and New Orleans where our clients and employees immersed themselves in the leading edge of pop culture provided the high-octane fuel for our creative engine. On each journey we cultivated collaborative relationships with the front-runners—graffiti and hip hop artists, avant-guard filmmakers, curators of fashion, political strategists, journalists, futurists, psychiatrists, screenwriters, actors, musicians, drama coaches, performance artists, chaos theory physicists, corporate titans, entrepreneurs, congressman, technologists, toy designers. Ideas flowed, perspectives changed, and new fusions emerged in our work, including the way everyone saw business problems and new possibilities for imaginative solutions. Our creative thinking skills expanded in speed, flexibility and ingenuity. The discovery mindset slid easily into the daily fabric of our business, as everyday interactions became sources of new ideas and new discoveries.

## A sixth sense

Discovery brings the vitality and virility of wonder into the organization. A sixth sense. We also gain inquisitiveness and enduring emotional bonds from engaging and sharing in the strange and the unknown together, as well as courage for bringing new ideas back into what we are doing. Discovery brings with it a positive flow; nothing is wasted and we benefit from it all.

**5**

# *Story*

*Members of the Swedish Academy, ladies and gentlemen, narrative has never been merely entertainment for me. It is, I believe, one of the principal ways in which we absorb knowledge. I hope you will understand then why I begin these remarks with the opening phrase of what must be the oldest sentence in the world and the earliest one we remember from childhood, "Once upon a time."*

—Toni Morrison, accepting the 1993
Nobel Prize for Literature

Story, which has its root in the word "storehouse," is the best vessel we have for holding values, identity, purpose, and personality. It is the foundation for vision. Knowing our stories gives us a wealth of identity and powerful kinds of knowing; and telling our stories leads to understanding and deep communication. A leader's responsibility is to perpetuate vision and seed the next generation of stories from the wealth of the storehouse. The outcome of skillful use of story is a synergistic leveraging of assets and a healthy sense of differentiation.

## The storehouse: knowing what we have

The vision of corporate leaders is cloudy because our stories are being lost. Big conglomerates have grown so large they can't feel their extremities any more. As *New York Times* columnist Thomas Friedman puts it, "If Seaman's only knew what Seaman's knows." [1] In their frenzied rush to jump on the next acquisition bandwagon, organizations become so unwieldy they don't know what they have or how to use it. They undervalue and often openly disrespect the history, experience, and tradition of individuals and organizations they have acquired, as well as the company they used to be. Valuable learning from the experiments of past administrations becomes easy political fodder, rather than valuable insights from which to grow.

When organizations consolidate, they erase whole companies, veins of talent, history, connections, and know-how that they do not even realize they have. It's not only that they don't know the faces of their individual employees, they don't know the ground these employees have covered collectively: the dead ends, discoveries, pitfalls, and break-throughs they have survived. In their carefully tabulated exchange of material, buildings, information, client lists, and employees, they often miss their greatest intangible resource—the stories that will outlive them all.

## Elusive synergies

It's no wonder synergies so rarely happen. In the modern corporate world the word synergy is supposed to mean 1+1=3, but more often it turns into -3. The one side of the equation does not know what the other is worth, much less who they are. Strategic "analysis" gives the illusion of rigor and understanding, but the high failure rate of M&A belies the truth. We have to start seeing the possibilities beyond the spreadsheets and logos.

The failed formula is too familiar: strategically envision grand synergies (that most often prove illusionary and unworkable), overpay by a sizable premium, overestimate the cost savings by throwing one management team out, and underestimate the ensuing poor performance. In a cost-cutting frenzy, throw more people out, further eroding performance and morale, fumble the potential benefits of integration, because you don't really know the product lines or the clients or the people, then make another acquisition quick before the shareholders are on to you.[2] There you have it, the new M&A math, 1+1= -3. A real factor in the disappointing results of many mergers is the failure of the surviving leaders to recognize the value of corporate story and culture as an asset and competitive advantage.

Having failed to learn their own stories, leaders cannot possibly hear the stories of the culture they're merging into. You learn your story by listening to mine, reacting and revising. That's how stories get shared: *You ate fish sticks on Friday nights? We always had pizza. Really? We stopped getting pizza the night my dad found out my sister was going out with the Domino's boy . . .* Narrative begets narrative, and when time is invested in the ongoing exchange, rich unexpected stories emerge. Without the investment of time and the shaping by storytellers, misunderstood cultures are often force-fitted together, and their assets become unrecognizable. Newly merged companies lose sight of who they've been and who they might become; they lose the thread of a story that might lead them back to it.

Story is necessary because stories are composed of the stuff we attach activity and emotion to, time and place, people and personalities, actions and reactions, arrivals and leave-takings, beginnings and endings. Without a story, we can't get up in the morning; we can't make decisions; we don't know who we are. Multiply this on a collective scale, and you can see the real problem facing so many corporations today. From Greek mythology to Native American art, cultures have sustained themselves by storytelling. When cared for well, stories are an organization's most enduring asset, undiminished by use and sharpened by time.

## Knowing what we know—stories as differentiators

If the essence of discovery is knowing what we don't know, then the essence of story is knowing what we know—a necessary contradiction. With endless industry consolidation as the prevailing response to global complexity and speed, mega-companies have become, as T George Harris tells us, "Gifted at economies of scale, but unable to use the scope of their knowledge to create the new products and systems needed in the business environment now emerging." We simply do not know what we know.

Think of the potential we miss in today's companies because we do not know what we've got. The Wright Brothers, two mechanics from Dayton, Ohio, solved a problem that had trumped humankind since Leonardo da Vinci. "A challenge that had fascinated man since before mythology had been licked by two tinkers who put their machine together using bicycle parts," says Kirk Varnedoe. "In the spirit of invention, they transformed the world by using what lay at hand, by seeing in parts kicking around the shop the potential that would change everything."

> **The essence of story is knowing what we know.**

Story is the programming language of culture, the software that runs the hardware. It informs and governs the way we interpret reality. An organization's stories live in its culture and vice-versa. Like petri dishes in a biology lab, a rich culture is especially conducive to the flourishing of growth. Growing from the roots of our cultures, stories reflect our highest core values, our beliefs, and our future visions. They house the symbols, the contexts, connections, observations, and questions that have built the company. They are the central nervous system of our framework for understanding—the core that defines us and continues to inform us today.

Visionary leaders bestow something of their character upon their companies, but as an organization grows, the founder's voice and defining story grow fainter. In the end, organizations draw their stories from their members. In the industrial world of overnight product imitation, an ever-increasing situation in the Age of Ideas, the richness of an organization's culture illuminated by its stories will be valuable equity and a potent differentiator.

The stacks of documents that name, legislate, and direct our businesses give us the illusion that we have our own corporate story nailed down, but our need of verbal story-telling is no less acute than the Greek sailor or the Native American child. When we don't have an accessible sense of our real story, we have to borrow cheesy imitations from the media or steal them from our competitors. We need to listen to our own stories and pay attention to the wealth of identity we have in those storehouses, not just to use them as marketing ploys but so we can know who we are and how to be in the world.

In today's info-glut, our access to information is escalating at a faster rate than our ability to organize it and attach meaning to it. Whereas a few years ago we were awed by new portals of information and technology, those inseparable twins of cyberspace, their proliferation now seems epidemic. Even a good thing, when rendered mammoth, becomes the stuff of nightmares. By some accounts, the production of knowledge is growing at a rate of 50% per year, while our capacity for consumption is remaining relatively the same.[3]

We all need to develop nimbler mental mechanisms for sifting and attaching the facts, for interpreting and cohering knowledge. The material in our minds is organized through complex bundles: images, maps, pictures, sensual experiences, numbers, and metaphors, but their capacity to hold complexity is more limited than that of stories. Stories are the heavy lifters of mental activity, with an expansive capacity for both material and meaning. However, because we digest stories so easily and carry them so lightly, we often fail to recognize the scope of their power.

## Stories: sharpening our capacity to learn

We remember things better through stories. There is something extravagant about the breadth of a story's web for catching meaning and for focusing value. For years it has been known that objective tests, though simpler to grade, are less effective than essay tests for demonstrating learning. So, for instance, a test that asks for the dates of Hitler's invasion of Poland demands less cognitive activity than an essay question asking for the three main results of Hitler's invasion of Poland.

What educators now realize is that both types of questions are far less capacious than a narrative question, one that asks us to put ourselves in the story, "What would you do if you were living in Poland when Hitler invaded?" Contrary to the great myth of objectivity, thinking narratively and personally usually makes us smarter.

On our first day with a new organization, we come home with handbooks and folders full of policies and information. They are part of the supply-side of the organization's knowledge. But the way we really learn and attach information in our first days in a new organization is through the stories we hear: *This is how HCV Inc. has been for me. This is something I'd never do again. . .* Those stories will serve as the information skeleton for all of the data you take in from then on unless you come up against a stronger story. Organizations need to think carefully about what stories they are telling, particularly in times of change.

## Story as guide

Working with the furniture industry, I had good opportunities for observing the way people buy furniture. Couples set out full of hope and affection to select their purchases. They drive to the showroom, wander around the maze of possibilities, sitting on love seats and stretching out in recliners. All goes well until it's time to order. Then they go into the order room where there are three thousand fabric samples to choose from, eight different wood finishes, three different levels of stain resistance, multiple arm and leg configurations, ticking options, and on and on. They become overwhelmed. They have no idea what kind of sofa arm they want, much less what kind their partner really wants or her mother thinks they should have, much less what kind of fabric the children they do not even yet have will need. By this point, they're beginning to feel more inclined to get a divorce than a sofa. Why is the whole process so unnerving? Story as a guide can help.

The words furniture and family both come from the Latin word *familiars* which refers to the essentials—the pots, pans and stools—the nomads carried with them as they migrated from place to place. Little wonder buying furniture is such an emotional experience. We are not simply choosing a sofa, we are choosing our *familiars*, the things we will carry with us, the things that will give shape and beauty and comfort to our lives. In some ways buying furniture is more like adoption than acquisition. It demands that we envision the chapters of our life we haven't yet lived. It demands that we know our own story.

What customers really need is not more information, but help in imagining their own stories. At pivotal times in our organizational lives we need to be especially attentive to the shape and power of our stories.

All of us have been a part of this process in times of crisis. *There's been a misunderstanding; now we all need to get our stories straight!* When things get tense we try to re-align the ambiguities of the story—an appropriate approach, because stories have a will and way of their own, and if they aren't addressed they can be as toxic as they are beautiful. But, the great untapped resource of stories lies not in controlling their power, but in using their power for growth.

### Stories as capital

Jim Thompson is a guy who knows his story. The afterthought child of a large, partying family, Jim was just six years old when his mother died. Raised with a generous rein by Daddy Jack, his fun-loving, Epicurean father, Jim grew up watching three football games at a time on the TVs stacked on top of each other in his living room, ordering lobster and French fries from menus around the world, and mixing great Black Russians and Golden Cadillacs. By the time he left Indiana for the University of Arizona, Jim had learned much from his dad.

Daddy Jack died unexpectedly during the first weeks of Jim's freshman year. Eight years later Jim returned to Indianapolis, got his big sister to co-sign a loan on restaurant space in a rundown strip mall near the family home, and started *Daddy Jack's*.[4] He drew from a well of good will and deep affection as he got underway. His brother sat down with a beer and wrote the menu, naming everything on it after members of his family, from Mean Jean's Onion Rings to Sweet Sexy Suzy's Succulent Salad. His cousins stripped and polished the floors; his Aunt Carole hung family pictures; and his Aunt Jeanne signed on as hostess. In the first year of operation, revenue reached one million dollars. Two years later, Jim rented the space next door to Daddy's and opened *Kona Jack's*, the best sushi bar and widest array of fresh and salt-water fish in the Midwest. Later he opened *Deli Jack's* one door down, then finally bought the entire shopping center and added the last jewel to the crown: *Après Jack's*, a lavish cigar and cognac bar with live music and big fireplace to brighten Indianapolis winters.

> **How does someone develop this kind of cultural capital selling seafood at the corner of two interstates in the heart of corn country?**

With its four distinct spaces, formats, and themes, the genius of the group is that it is not a chain. Each restaurant draws from the central Daddy Jack's philosophy, ideology, and mythology, but allows the personality of the chefs and staff, as well as the clientele in each place to interpret that philosophy in their own authentic way. Today the successful restaurants dwarf industry statistics, with no sign of recession anywhere.

How does someone develop this kind of cultural capital selling seafood at the corner of two interstates in the heart of corn country? The food is good and the décor is good enough, but the magic of Daddy Jack's comes from knowing its story and from communicating the story from the parking lot to the kitchen. The menu tells the tale:

*Welcome to Daddy Jack's*

> *Did you notice the big red Cadillac parked curbside in front of the restaurant? It belongs to Daddy Jack.*
>
> *To know Daddy Jack, you have to think big: Big shoulders, big heart, big plans. And, of course, a big finely tuned appetite for excellent food and generous drinks.*
>
> *Restaurants past and present are marked prominently on Daddy Jack's life map. From the old Tee Pee on 38th Street to the Corner Tavern on the shores of Lake Maxinkuckee, from Caesar's Palace Court on the Vegas Strip to Dorian's on the Kona Coast, Daddy Jack has adopted the best and most unique as his own and brought it here to North Meridian.*
>
> *Eating and drinking aren't necessities in the world according to Daddy Jack. They are pleasures woven inextricably into his code of life, which goes something like this: Live life fully, play to win, share the spoils of victory, have lots of laughs. And always, always, remember your friends.*
>
> *So consider yourself a friend of Daddy Jack's. Relax, have a drink, maybe a meal, catch a game on TV, and share a few laughs. Daddy Jack will take good care of you.*
>
> *Put this place on your life's road map, and hurry back. But please don't park by the curb.*
>
> *That space is reserved for Daddy Jack.*

Like any businessperson in a tough economy, Jim Thompson has had plenty of hard decisions to make: how to advertise, how to innovate, how to manage, and how to keep growing. But unlike many, he has resources for answering hard questions. Surrounded by the stories and culture that have grounded his work, he reaches back to deep resources and clear guidance. Jim's eyes well with pride as he looks around the restaurant covered with pictures of his dad and mom, grandparents, aunts, uncles, cousins, brothers, and sisters. He loves his story and invites everyone who enters his business place to be part of it.

Unlike slogans or rhymes, stories begin with time and place. They work, not because they're coy or clever or even remarkable. They work, because they're true. Begin with the details and let them take you to the center. Storytelling works best for small businesses, for entrepreneurs who know themselves and their audiences well; but large corporations can tap into it as well. The employees at Wal-Mart would recognize Sam Walton's truck as easily as the diners at Daddy's recognize Daddy's red Cadillac. Companies with a good story are able to true up their many little stories by returning to the details of their big story over and over again.

## Guinness storehouse

An ocean away in Dublin, at the venerable Guinness Company's new headquarters called The Storehouse, we studied the work of a large canvas storyteller, Ralph Ardill, and his design team from Imagination in London. A communications grand master, Ardill learned the challenge of telling an evolving live story by marketing rock stars for CBS Records in London. By comparison, selling a century-old company seems relatively easy: "At least here, we are working with a product that is never going to tell you it doesn't like its new packaging. It's never going to say it's not turning up for that product launch. It's never going to go out and take drugs."

Ardill sees brands as people. They are multi-faceted and opinionated with many sides to their personality that make them vital, alive, and interesting. Like people, brands change throughout their lives; they evolve. Out of that evolution are born stories. One of the biggest mistakes that can be made in communicating a story is to keep telling the same one over and over in the same way. The Beatles had a lot of equity in the song "A Hard Days Night," but they moved on. So must companies.

Guinness, the makers of the Irish ale that is now consumed world-wide at the rate of 10,000,000 daily servings, had lost ground in the critically important youth market, even in Ireland. Says Ardill, "Guinness wanted to reconnect to young Irish people, some of whom were rejecting it. In their eyes, it stands for a lot of the things that are negative in their world—old-fashioned tradition, the starkness of the product, the fact that it was their fathers' drink is something that encourages a lot of drinkers to switch off and not make themselves available to the brand."

Imagination, together with Irish architecture firm RKD and a team from Guinness, set out to reconnect the brand with its social roots that are all about people having a good time together. But rather than a themed brand experience or a Guinness Cathedral, they created a real community. On any given day at The Storehouse, there are people who work nearby coming to the bar for a sandwich for lunch, employees who have flown in from all over the world for a Guinness training course, tourists who want to experience the Guinness story, and people who have come just to see an exhibition in the art gallery.

The Guinness space does not tell its great story in a reductive or deductive fashion, but is intuitive and intriguing. There is a quality of freedom that encourages exploration. A spectacular cascading 30-meter indoor waterfall conveys the power and importance of water to the brewing process. Says Ardill, "We tried to create messages and sensations for people that would allow you and me to be in the same space, looking at the same waterfall, walking through it and our take-aways would be different. This reflects a fundamental shift where brands now have to look at how  they can find a place in the lives of people rather than trying to create places where people can live in their world."

The team thoughtfully chose to introduce Guinness's new story to the world by hosting an opening night for Dublin's young adult crowd, no VIPs. They resisted the temptation to have a black tie gala. "If we had opened it that way," says Ardill, "the image the next day would have been of the Prime Minister of Ireland having a pint in the bar on the roof, which would have given all the wrong signals."

This kind of humanization of story, brands, and organizations impacts every aspect of corporate behavior and communication.

> **There has never been more pressure on companies and brands to develop relationships and be human.**

There has never been more pressure on companies and brands to develop relationships and be human. The paradox is that companies are preaching relationships—portfolios, cradle to grave—while practicing intrusion. "There's a watershed coming where brands are going to have to provide more intuitive and intriguing communication that makes us want to go to it and seek it out and make it a part of our lives rather than impose itself in our lives," says Ardill.

### Storytelling

We all need to lean into our stories, to tell them well, and re-fresh them often with new stories. We need to remember that consumers don't see our careful research, concise briefs, and efficient media plans. They see our story and it either moves them or it doesn't. Stories are the thing we all have plenty of, but use too thoughtlessly. We can dull the central resources of our company's culture by the ways we conceive and tell our stories. Or we can attend to them and grow them as our unique and most consummately replenishable source for growth.

# 6

# *Conversation*

*For millions of years, mankind lived just like the animals. Then something happened which unleashed the power of our imagination. We learned to talk, we learned to listen. Speech has allowed the communication of ideas enabling human beings to work together. To build the impossible. Mankind's greatest achievements have come about by talking...talking...talking. And it's greatest failures, by not talking. It doesn't have to be like this. Our greatest hopes could become reality and the future, with the technology at our disposable, the possibilities are unbounded. All we need to do is make sure we keep talking... talking... talking.*

—Stephen Hawkings

Conversation is the best tool we have for managing ideas and galvanizing the resources necessary to turn them into action. It is more than the thing we do when we are not working. It is the work itself. Individuality, at its best, is grown from and plowed back into the common soil of community. The process of the exchange that ultimately leads to growth is conversation.

Conversation thrives when leaders demonstrate their own ability for transformational dialogue, entering into the exchange expecting to turn, expecting to change, and expecting to grow. Leaders need to read broadly and deeply, not only the work of their own field, but diverse fields as well. What's more, they need to become broad and deep readers of people. The payoff will be an organization with the capacity to gather resources, honor individuality, exchange ideas and skills effectively; and to reproduce. In short, it will grow.

## Establishing the commons

To a person, all of the mad dogs and sages we've studied have an extraordinary gift for conversation. Each one delights in the commerce of words, the exchange of ideas in the common space of conversation, and expects that space to have changed when they leave it. Charged with the available ions of ideas, they bring the open environment of the commons with them wherever they go.

Since colonial days, the American enterprise has been committed to fostering individualism in an environment of ongoing and universally accessible conversation.[1]   This is a phenomenon we must perpetuate in the Age of Ideas.  Unlike the European village that existed to support the landowner's estate, early American villages were organized around a physical commons, an architecture of town life that put the well, the grazing lands, and places of exchange at the center of the community. Each settler was expected to defend the common sources they shared.[2]

Of course, urbanization everywhere has blurred many national distinctions, but in small towns, they are still evident. In the Latin America *hacienda*, the gaiety of family life is surrounded by walls, as are the gardens of Europe and Asia. But in small towns in the U.S., life still happens *towards* the street—front yards, sidewalks, and porch swings. There is the ongoing expectation of shared life in city squares, public soccer fields, libraries, playgrounds, and national parks.

For an organization to support vital conversation, it must have a *commons*, owned by no one and accessible to all. Protecting the commons, this shared area of resources, knowledge and access, is a vital responsibility of leadership.

## Intellectual commons

Besides the physical design of her villages, America has always protected the commons of intellectual and cultural sources, a free flow of ideas and conversation open to all. Because early copyright laws were not internationally enforceable, early American printing presses were able to make the great writers of England available to common people cheaply and easily. For American writers and inventors, copyrights and patents were cheap and easy to obtain, supporting individual discovery. But their duration was short, so that each generation of thinkers inherited the same range of possibilities for success.

The great dangers to innovation are a consolidation of ownership leading to loss of independent and spontaneous relationships, increasingly restrictive intellectual property laws leading to a narrowing of the commons of ideas, and executive arrogance leading to dishonesty and the blockade of ports of communication. More than any gift to the future of innovation in the Age of Ideas a generous seeding of opportunities for intimate conversation without the burden of hierarchy will assure diverse and sustainable growth in American thought and productivity.

## Transformational conversation: "turning together"

Essential to the art of thinking is the art of juxtaposing—of holding unlike images or ideas together in meaningful dialogue without one side misreading or eclipsing the other. By that definition, we should be living in the golden age of thinking. In a world of web-surfing, Kazaa, downloading, and split screens, our capacity to juxtapose images, texts, sounds, and numbers is quantum. However, when it comes to making new connections, our technological capacity for juxtaposition is not as agile as a pair of human minds. Whether in royal courts or in board rooms, on front porches or on basement sofas, the most efficient and productive means we have today for juxtaposing and connecting continues to be human conversation.

Though most of the people we interviewed are accomplished writers and public speakers, they seem most fully alive in dialogue. Neither debaters nor entertainers when they speak, they are engagers. For them, dialogue is not the stage on which thought is expressed; it is the cradle in which thought is born.

**Essential to the art of thinking is the art of juxtaposing—of holding unlike images or ideas together in meaningful dialogue**

As Nancy Beach says, "I used to believe that ministry was what you did after you finished all your difficult conversations; now I realize that ministry *is* the difficult conversations. And that who I am is, to some extent, a result of all those difficult conversations." Innovators don't *present* themselves in conversation, they *become* themselves.

## The dangers of limiting conversation—Vietnam

Former Secretary of Defense Robert McNamara used his book *In Retrospect: The Tragedy and Lessons of Vietnam* to address the biggest leadership question of twentieth-century: How did we get it so wrong in Vietnam?"[3] Relying on contemporaneous documents—notes of meetings, memoranda, and personal letters—he comes to the conclusion that although every person at the table of leadership had enough information to know that the course of escalation during the last years of the war was disastrous, there was no appropriate way to say it. So they kept their insights and reservations to themselves.

"Why?" asks McNamara in his memoir. "Most people wish to avoid confrontation. They preferred to finesse disagreement rather than to address it head-on. Also, I speculate that LBJ, like all presidents, wanted to avoid an open split among his key subordinates, especially during wartime. So he swept our divergence of opinion under the rug. It was a very human reaction."

During the Vietnam War there was no commons at the table of leadership. At that critical time, the leaders of the United States were fundamentally unable to talk, to listen, to talk back, to hear, and to imagine—even as the situation grew more desperate. They were simply unable to converse, to *turn together*. This turning together is the root of conversation; it assumes a million little points of revision, changing our words, changing our tones, changing our minds and it assumes changing our assumptions as well. When we converse, we agree to the possibility of change.

## Being well-read and reading well

Another commonality among our mad dogs and dreamers is a passion for reading, both deeply in their own fields and broadly across diverse fields and from uncommon sources. Besides reading with intention and attention, they read books with great pleasure, and they seem to read people the same way.

Reading is one of our best disciplines for insight. It requires a rigorous grappling with the ambiguity found in the spaces between intention, reception, and interpretation, whether we are reading the words on a page or the lives of those around us. It is our ability to embrace ambiguity, to step in and out of context, to empathize and analyze, to anticipate and rethink, to name and reflect that makes us good readers.

Much more than the decoding of symbols, reading is the making of meaning. We bring as much to reading as we take away from it, and an engaged awareness of the transaction is essential for honest and productive exchange. We are deeply affected by who and what we read, but we are equally effected by the way we are read by others. The power of good reading moves both ways. As we take care to read our colleagues, projects, and resources better, we can read them and ourselves into growth.

When we read, we don't read every word, one after another. Rather, as we read any text, we make infinite mental decisions about how to penetrate the words within it. If we are simply looking for information, we skim the surface, latching on to the key words or phrases we want to harvest. Even when we are reading for meaning, we don't read every word.

As readers, we naturally and unconsciously begin the process of understanding a text by dividing it into many little bite-size pieces of meaning—usually about five to eight words long. We chew them for meaning, while at the same time, tearing off the next piece. When a piece doesn't go down easily, we back up, pick it up in another cluster and have another go at it. Instruments called tachistoscopes track this process; they record the actions of the eye and mind as they pick up a cluster of words, guess at its meaning, reread it and revise it. *Guess and revise*—that's the basic formula for insightful reading.

## Reading people well

It's also the basic formula for an insightful reading of another person. We've all encountered individuals who fail to make any guesses about who we are and what we have to say to them. They may speak to us, even ask polite questions, but they are not engaged or invested enough to be affected by our answers. It is as if every aspect of our encounter slides by them.

On the other hand, we've all met people who are vigorous guessers, sizing us up the minute we shake hands. But, they seem unable to revise their assessment of us, no matter how much evidence piles up against their initial guess.

Finally, we've all met good readers of people, whose warmth and curiosity lead them to ask us thoughtful questions and to reframe their ongoing questions and comments in light of our responses. Readers who guess and revise well offer us the gift of feeling truly known.

To be read by another person with empathy and insight is a deeply satisfying experience, and the regenerative effect it has on both the reader and the one who is read is the often-undeveloped locus of mutual growth.

In many work situations, leaders have unique opportunities for reading their colleagues and employees well. They see individuals in their daily interactions, and they see the big sweep of activity and conversation those individuals generate and move toward. Business leaders may not have enough information to understand fully what new employees are saying in their actions, comments, reports, and petitions, but they have enough to begin the process of guessing and revising to insure that the employee *ensure?* knows he will be read with care and insight.

Many of the mad dogs we interviewed attributed their own growth and success to the insight of a leader who saw possibility in them as new colleagues or apprentices and told them what they were guessing. A good leader who reads us well is the one who can put a finger on who we are and where we are going and takes the time to do so.

The leaders in our study reported that the mentors in their lives were imaginative and piercing readers, willing to guess big and revise quickly as they read them toward greatness. There is nothing more dispiriting for a colleague or an employee than to be *overlooked* or *under-read* by a leader. We all can tell the difference between being skimmed and being read.[4]

In an era when we are well aware of our capacity to *get it wrong,* to make embarrassing assumptions about one another in regard to gender, race, or class, we must work diligently at the discipline of actively reading the lives and words of those with whom we work. In order to play it safe, to avoid the embarrassment of making unexamined or biased assumptions, we may refuse to assume anything at all.

Since we cannot think without assumptions, the trick is not to deny our assumptions, but to get them on the table, honestly and tentatively, and to be quick to trade them in for better assumptions as soon as they come up short. That's the hard work of active and meaningful reading—guessing big and revising constantly.

As the people we work with come to believe we will read them with pleasure, interpret them meaningfully, and envisage them generously, they become less self-protective, giving more expansive clues to their needs and more energy to their work.

Should we read people's lives out loud? Isn't there a danger of over-interpreting if we articulate the guesses we are making out loud? We don't think so. It is when we make private, isolated guesses about people's motives and expressions that our assumptions about them start to calcify and distort. If we are to envisage a person, we must do it as we go along, easily and lightly, with constant attention to adjustment based on their revealing of themselves by the ongoing clues they give us.

**In the near future, our current systems of assessment will seem as outdated and ineffective as dunce caps.**

Many of the traditional systems of assessment in today's companies—commissions, incentive plans, and the year-end review are being reconsidered in the light of a recent discoveries about intrinsic motivation and the impact of different types of feedback.[5]

In the near future, our current systems of assessment will seem as outdated and ineffective as dunce caps. Meanwhile, we all need to read one another better. Assessment, a word that literally means *sitting together*, should be an ongoing dialogue. To do it well requires a two-way process, getting and giving a good read.

## The mad dog and the sage

Dan Yankelovich is not only an expert on the subject of conversation—he is a genius in the art of it. Held in highest respect by leaders from all corners of America, Yankelovich has been a consultant for the State of the Union Address by every president since Nixon.[6] As Bill Moyers puts it, "I know of no one better equipped to help us talk to each other as citizens. Daniel Yankelovich is the best listener I know. Because he has been listening to America for so long now, he hears the hopes and fears, anxieties and aspirations that are often lost in anger, ambiguity, or haste."

Our visit with Yankelovich took place on a warm spring morning in T George Harris's San Diego backyard. Yankelovich had strolled over from his house just up the street, and as we sat talking around a well-worn redwood table among the bougainvillea and snapdragons, we sensed the legacy of great conversations and insight that had been forged there.

Having grown up in the advertising and marketing world, I have great respect for the venerable *Yankelovich Monitor* which has had its finger on the pulse of American public opinions, feelings, and values for over thirty years. The oracle for many of the world's leading companies, institutions and governments, the *Yankelovich Monitor* has not only been the definitive source of public opinion, it has broken ground for a whole new profession of tracking social, political, and economic trends and measuring shifts in people's values and beliefs.

This morning, Yankelovich is dressed in a white Australian bush hat and large dark horn rim glasses. Solidly built with large hands and a joyous laugh, like a Koala bear in the bush, Yankelovich is a gentle, compassionate, and thoughtful man who observ' everything with keen perception. His curious, searching intellect misses nothing. Having spent his life studying the ways millions of people think and act, Yankelovich is unusually at home in himself and agile in his ability to create a common ground for conversation.

He and Harris are like two fisherman eager to get their poles in. And the catch is breathtaking. The scope and connections of the conversations are dazzling, coursing with piercing question, wry observation, and real exchange through the Kennedy years, the transformation of Bob McNamara, Donald Rumsfeld's need to reformulate, the global missteps at Coke, the effects of 9/11, fallout at the Red Cross. . .

Then on to the new role of boards following the Enron debacle, re-establishing trust and the post 9/11 psyche of America, the implications of the aging of the population, the changing role of government, the global market economy, social learning, health care reform in America and Canada, product innovation, politics, economics, finance, advertising, Indonesian fundamentalism, false paradises, the SAT, military strategy, NASA, homeland defense, …with tremendous clarity they see the patterns and flows of complex phenomena in context and at a glance. It is nothing short of staggering that he and T George not only conversed in a way that let us ride with them, they allowed us to *drive*.

## The magic of dialogue

After years of observation and experimentation, as well as by triangulating his findings with scholars from other fields, Yankelovich has come to believe in a process of dialogue. Through dialogue we arrive at a different kind of truth than we arrive at analytically or through scientific experiments.

Yankelovich has noticed that it takes the public a long time to arrive at a considered judgment. In this world of split-second information bombardment, our ability to absorb, comprehend, and consider often takes decades. For example, offers Yankelovich, it took years for Americans to decide that committed internationalism, for all its drawbacks, was better for our nation than isolationism. It took decades for America to feel comfortable with women working outside the home, to accept the victims of AIDS as worthy of help, to decide that a woman would be acceptable as President.

"If you share frameworks in common," says Yankelovich, "if you come from the same culture, language, organization, share the same experiences, then ordinary conversation is a very good vehicle for communication." He continues:

With a shared framework, ordinary conversation permits you to be in touch with one another. This is becoming increasingly rare in our society. We are in an era of specialization where almost everybody you meet has a different framework than you. Then ordinary conversation doesn't permit you to understand one another. You need to go to a greater effort.

Yankelovich sees dialogue as a unique kind of discourse, utilizing special skills to achieve two results. First, it seeks a deeper level of thought through mutual understanding. Second, it cultivates a richer level of feeling through mutual respect and trust. The process of dialogue, he explains, engages people at a profound level of depth, openness, and empathy. Learning from these perspectives is best informed to shape leadership and judgment. With the right kind of dialogue the process of considered judgments on complex issues can be accelerated, a critical asset in a time-crunched world.

Important to an understanding of the power of dialogue is insight into the nature of how the public learns and forms judgment.

Yankelovich sees four forms of learning that go on simultaneously:

1. Conveying information, something the media does very well
2. Seeing something in a new light, connecting the dots, having an insight
3. Dealing with hard choices, which takes time. Because we usually avoid talking about tradeoffs, we haven't developed skills at recognizing them
4. Looking at things beyond an individual point of view, what's in it for me—shifting to how can *we* deal with this problem

"One of the best ways to understand dialogue is to contrast it to debate," says Yankelovich.

> Debate is about winning, attempting to prove the other side wrong. It is about defending your assumptions and views against the other side. In debate the mindset is to search for flaws and weakness in the others' position, and listen to make counter-arguments ultimately seeking an outcome that agrees with your position. It is combative.
>
> Dialogue is collaborative. It is about finding common ground, understanding, and searching for the strength and value in others' positions. By admitting that other's thinking can improve your own and listening to understand and find a basis for agreement, you discover new possibilities and opportunities.
>
> Ultimately, dialogue prepares the ground for negotiation or decision-making on emotionally laden issues.

As Yankelovich spoke, it became clear how rare genuine dialogue is in both our personal lives and our work lives. At the time of our encounter with him, Yankelovich was working on a project for the Canadian government—a formal dialogue session —as they decided on their next era of health care. He explained:

> The government is trying to reform the health care system that has been eroding in recent years, and it's something that Canadians feel passionately about because in their mind, it's one of the things that distinguishes them from the barbarians in the south.
>
> The disconnect we found is that these are government officials, bureaucrats, and experts of various sorts. They think in terms of principals of governance, efficiency, and budgets where people are thinking in terms of What do you do when you're sick? What kind of health care do you need for yourself and your family?[7]

We were impressed; Yankelovich was talking about helping Canada work through healthcare as if she were a neighbor borrowing a cup of sugar. Could he have helped Hillary? "Well," he smiles, "we were actually working on a formal deliberation for the U.S. healthcare system when Bill Clinton took office. One of the rules of dialogue, however, is that everyone has to agree to leave their original agenda and assumptions at the door. Hillary Clinton already knew what she wanted for American healthcare reform in 1993, and—to her credit, really—she knew she wouldn't leave it at the door. We cancelled the dialogue."

More than throwing power around at a board meeting or impressing a group with his stunning access to statistics and trends, it is clear why Yankelovich has spent his life studying conversation. He loves the discovery it yields and the growth that it fosters.

"In a great dialogue you feel that you have reached out and touched and heard and felt another human being so that you have really transcended the limitations of living within your own skin," he says. "That sense of intimacy and the satisfaction that comes from it is so fundamental and so primitive, I think it's something that's wired in. There is a sense of satisfaction that people get, a sense of community, a sense of belongingness."

We spent an amazing day conversing with Dan Yankelovich in a Mary Poppins kind of sweep through the countryside: seeing a breadth of issues, people, and perspectives in a new light. After lunch and more talk, he tipped his bush hat and started up the driveway as undramatically as he'd come. Then he stopped and turned back for a minute. Looking at us with the exuberance of a kid, he said, "Thanks. I enjoyed the talk. You all are extraordinary." Of course, that's the secret to the good conversation—finding overlap between the disparate, seeing the extraordinary in everyone, enjoying the process, and expecting to grow from it.

# 7

# *Contradiction*

*Do I contradict myself?*
*Very well, then I contradict myself,*
*I am large, I contain multitudes.*

—Walt Whitman

Contradictions are portals for sustainable growth. They spark new innovations through unlikely connections of knowledge. As a tool, they can help us develop a more fluent and prismatic way of seeing that expands our sense of possibility. Sustainable growth through seeing new connections requires active diversity, cross-fertilization, and improvisation. The role of leadership is to build divergent elements into the organization, for sustained idea combustion. Out of that comes new opportunities, fresh ideas, and growth through innovation.

Contradictions in business, as in life, generally have a negative connotation. How often have you heard *You've contradicted yourself!* or *That's a contradiction!* or *Don't contradict me!?* The conventional use of the word implies disagreement, opposition, discrepancy, denial, poor judgment, and even conflict. Most businesses (and people) fear the discord contradictions may evoke. It has the potential to negate the hoped for answers, the party line, or the way we've always done it before. Companies find contradictions so unsettling they actively organize them out.

By restricting flows of information and access to the overall plan, *need-to-know* management is able to suppress ideas that may contradict those plans. Nothing is more repressive than lack of information, the inability to gain topographical perspective of the terrain. A significant part of every totalitarian regime has been a rationing of information. Flow charts that map the permissible conversations in the organization, stifling corporate cultures that narrow what is acceptable, and management that continually hire in its own image all contract vision and growth.

## Containing multitudes

The overlap between business and art, like those between the competing arenas of academics and religion, work and home, love and service, has vast potential for generating fresh energy, new ideas, and unrealized profit. Suspicion, however, keeps us blind to the possibilities as our preservation instinct trumps our intellectual curiosity. It hides behind the terms of purity, specialization, efficiency, or focus, but the real force is the fear of being wrong, or just of being unsettled. And so we ironically forfeit truth in order to avoid error. We must embrace contradiction in order to disarm our suspicion, and thereby loosen the bonds that restrain our growth.

## Cross-fertilization

Where do good ideas come from? Often, they come from the differences, from unlikely juxtapositions across disciplines of knowledge, from diversity and divergence of thought, from the provocative and genuinely new, and from intense engagement. Contradictions help spark and sharpen our imagination, intuition, and perceptiveness, they generate the new ideas, which become our next generation of growth.

Building paths for formal and informal cross-fertilization into the organization structure and culture is critical. As businesses reorganize around producing growth rather than fear of failure, cross-fertilization becomes a rich source of learning and invention. Building competencies in diverse fields, being present at the convergence points, and borrowing other lenses in order to bring a fuller range of vision to your own experience—this *amateur sleuthing* leads to fruitful hybridization.

Such intentional mixing of the professional expert and the amateur flies in the face of a tradition in corporate and academic thinking as old as the Industrial Revolution. In our urgency to master complex fields and processes, our direction is always toward the specifics, each person should know more about less. Since Remington's adoption of mass production in the last years of the Nineteenth century, we have focused on making things in parts. It works well for rifles and televisions, Barbies and hairdryers, but it doesn't work for everything. It doesn't always work for making space shuttles, as we saw with the Challenger, and it rarely works for making knowledge.

**Where do good ideas come from? Often, they come from the differences.**

Why? Real knowledge is not about just getting your piece right; it is about loving the way it's used. It sounds corny, but cross-fertilization works best when it's done out of love, when it is provoked, not by the professional who wants to download his expertise, but by the *amateur,* the one who is working out of love. Have you experienced the pleasure and insight that comes from talking with an amateur who is curious about your field? Enthusiastic questions by an amateur don't result in new details for the expert, but they can fan the flame of excitement and give a better focus for how the details you've been muddling around in for so long fit together.

We can all benefit from developing the amateur parts of our knowledge bank, our random acts of learning, not in order to ask the experts better questions, but in order to fit ourselves to the specific tasks of our own field. Specialization has resulted in a general "dumbing down." Recent discoveries in cognitive science have substantiated what renaissance thinkers have always known: the associational cortex of our brains (the part that recognizes and integrates disparate theories and new information) is the only part of the brain that continues to grow in vitality and effectiveness through middle life. The more we exercise it by stretching across contradictions and disciplines, the better our mind works.

As we consider this mandate to multiplicity in terms of the education and development of an individual, we also need to examine its implications for organizations. Management efforts towards cross-pollination—summit meetings, team teaching, shared leadership—need to take place on the front end, in overlap, interplay, and conversation *before* the project is defined.

## Robin Williams, not Bob Hope

Improvisation is a natural approach to today's fast pace of business. At the core of the creative process improvisation is about exploration and contradiction. The creative thinker arrives at the table not like Bob Hope with a memorized line and a trademark expression, but like Robin Williams with a manic wit and a mind prepared to respond to the opportunity that presents itself.

While Hope's mastery of the understatement and his predictability was the well-deserved comic relief of the World War II generation and the hard-working Industrial Age, Williams embraces the flamboyant, outrageous methods of the Age of Ideas. We need people to come to the conversation freely offering up concepts, points of view, ideas that are held lightly. Through contradictions in the midst of variety, you discover things you didn't anticipate; they become the new opportunities to build on.

To fully understand the power of improvisation, we need to debunk another myth of the creative process itself. As Joan Darling tells us, "When it looks the easiest, when it looks like you're winging it, it is actually the result of incredibly hard work and preparation. To improvise you have to have faith in the creative process. That, plus hundreds of hours of research, rigorous thinking, and intense engagement with the subject will make it cohesive. That's the responsible work of the creative process."

As the French poet Jacque Prevert said, "Chance doesn't occur by chance alone, but it does favor the prepared mind."

## Idea stages

*Idea stages* is a term we use to explain our approach for bringing divergent ideas, knowledge, and people together to inventively solve problems and create innovation. It starts by formulating a high level series of questions on a topic to pose to the organization as a whole. At LHC we held ongoing idea stages around broad subjects important to our clients and the growth of our business, such as *Rethinking Issues of Adolescence in America.*

Every person, including our vast network outside the agency, was encouraged to participate as we tackled an ongoing series of provocative questions and challenges, assessing unmet needs and motivational drivers. We searched for the most inventive thinkers on a subject inside and outside the company and invited them into the conversation. As we brought together people who were unfamiliar with each others' work, dialogue was stimulated and the distinctions and

**Through contradictions in the midst of variety, you discover things you didn't anticipate; they become the new opportunities to build on.**

discoveries at the intersections of these experiences gave birth to new ideas that fueled future growth.

## *Prismatic vision*

People see differently, they learn differently, they hear differently, and they comprehend differently. Rather than try to create an artificial corporate environment where all must try to do things the same way, we need to nurture environments where people are comfortable and accept differences as sources of strength, not weakness. New things will continuously and reliably emerge from the differences as we give ourselves opportunities to discover.

Shifting perspectives beyond the limitations of our discipline, industry, and conventions is liberating and emancipates us from the narrow rooms of our individual experience as it powers our imagination to conceive and revolutionize. Kirk Varnedoe commented:

> To get out of your rut and stop seeing the world the way other people see it, you can imaginatively project yourself outside the situation you're in and imagine you're looking at it from some other place. It is fundamental to our ability to reconceive, rethink, and re-imagine our situation.
>
> As Sir James Jeans, one of the greatest physicists of the twentieth century said, "The history of physical science in the twentieth century is one of emancipation from the purely human angle of vision." Einstein's theory of relativity had to do with imagining a structure from a system outside it. Never underestimate the ability of the mind to project itself outside of the situation and imagine the other.

## *Contradiction at work*

Encouraging cross-fertilization, connecting silos of knowledge, mining multiple disciplines for raw material, holding idea stages, working improvisationally, hiring and organizing for difference— these ultimately help us cultivate a new habit of mind. Rather than seeing and understanding opportunities or problems in one dimension, we can develop within the organization and within ourselves a series of lenses and filters—historic, economic, social, technical, artistic, environmental, political, and so on to enrich our understanding beyond the narrow spectrum and see the unlikely inter-relationships between them.

As futurist Alvin Toffler helps us understand, there is no unitary source of change. Change is always multi-causal, and the convergence and interaction of forces and counter forces create the waves of transformation and change. Contradiction and difference help us to ride and read them well.

# 8

# Voice

*Vocation. . . the place where our deep gladness
and the world's deep hunger meet.*

—Frederick Buechner

Voice. You can't buy it at the store, but it is fundamental to great business and inspiring leadership. It is the litmus test of organizational values. An environment that asks people to solve problems with rote efficiency, to do the same thing over and over, finds voice unnecessary and disruptive. An environment committed to the cultivation of new ideas, markets, products, processes, and services finds it productive. Voice is the variable that explodes the scarcity model of economics—when you use it, you end up with more, and everyone can use it.

What is voice? It's hard to define. Watch a Nike commercial or read a poem by Maya Angelou and you'll probably hear it; read the manual for your dishwasher and you probably won't. Bob Dole had it on *Saturday Night Live*; he didn't when he ran for President. It occurs more often in E-mail than in year-end reports, but it's not really related to form, nor is it governed by audience. It begins with one's ability to own oneself, and it grows with one's ability to give that self to the world. It thrives at the cusp of those two experiences.

Voice goes two ways. It's about learning to get in touch, listen to and trust your own instincts; it's about threading instinct and experience into the fulcrum of sharp, clear expression. Born at the intersection of tentativity and certainty, it requires both vulnerability and presence. It is the productive first ingredient for individuality and for collaboration, essential not only for changing the world, but for changing oneself.

**Voice. You can't buy it at the store, but it is fundamental to great business and inspiring leadership.**

Voice is an artesian well, the best resource of each person. Their most genuine, vital expression and energy, fueling the organization's best and wisest work. It happens when we are working at the center of our vocation—our calling, "the place where our own deep gladness meets the world's deep need."[1]

Leaders need to find their own voices, their own best resources for being genuine in the midst of their organization, and they need to invite and to host the fullest presence of their colleagues. To have voice is to be fully present, to feel counted in, and counted on, to have something to say, and to be heard. The payoff for working in an organization in which everyone brings real voice to their work is a full measure of energy, balance, understanding, and fun.

### Finding voice

One afternoon in Nairobi, I visited with a Masaii woman, a princess. Her father was the tribal chief, and she was one of a hundred brothers and sisters, children of his ten wives. I marveled at her sense of grace and dignity as we talked about growing up with ninety-nine siblings. Her husband came into the yard and as she walked over to meet him, she knelt down and swooped up a handful of grass. Later she explained, "A Masaii woman always offers grass before she speaks. How can you speak if you come empty-handed?"

A big part of finding our own voice is realizing that we don't come empty-handed. Unfortunately, in our urgency to bring something of our own to the workplace conversation, our reach is often too shallow. We offer the shrill voice of false confidence, the chatter of emptiness, the sigh of indifference, or the hollow echo of gossip. What is it then that we can swoop up before we speak to make our offering worthy?

We've all had moments when to our own surprise we find ourselves speaking with power and confidence about something we've thought about for a long time, but never thought we'd talk about. Or even more surprising, we find ourselves speaking with insight and conviction about something we never thought we'd care about in the first place.

Something provokes or engages us; a door gets opened and suddenly we begin to talk. Not small talk or business talk or chitchat, but real talk about things we've discovered, observed, and considered. The power of our own voice surprises us. Something has been turned on. We are now working and thinking in a faster, fuller way.

What happened? Usually one of two things. Either another person made it clear that he truly wanted to hear what we thought, or something inside of us decided it could not go on being unheard any longer. When we expect everyone to bring their handful of grass, we give one another permission to be heard.

Built into the fabric of many companies are an array of gestures, assumptions, and arrangements that give our whole work force a sense that what they have to bring to the feast is minimal or optional, or that it is only necessary on demand. We need full-spirited people, not sometimes, but all the time. We need to leave the power running. Imagine the magnification of energy and exchange. A family of a hundred princes and princesses reaping a rich harvest in a desert land!

### What makes voice real?

What makes for real talk? It's not certainty. In fact, if we know exactly what we're going to say, it may well be unreal, borrowed from old ideas or someone else's repertoire. When we feel unheard in a job or relationship, we begin talking to ourselves about it—too much. The words we don't get to say out loud get a grip on our mind. As we're mowing the grass or driving down the highway, we find ourselves rehearsing a litany of *should have saids* and *could have saids* over and over.

We imagine these words as the speech we're going to make in our exit interview, the final great truth we'll pronounce as we're walking out the door. But real truth doesn't get told that way. We cannot save up our real voice and best thoughts to drop in a neat package as we're leaving: *The extra disks are in the drawer, the keys are in the mailbox, and, by the way, I never liked the way you ran the office.*

> **Real voice is the experience of speaking and not leaving.**

Real voice is the experience of speaking and *not* leaving. Of saying what we know and feeling it ring true all the way down to our shoes, and continuing to stand in them. Of feeling strong as we stand and hearing the words and meanings that come back to us as we're standing strong in our own voice.

It involves not a turning away from power, responsibility, and community, but a turning toward it. It works as a centrifugal force, pulling all of our disparate ideas towards the center, rather than centripetal, casting them outward. It may begin with a whisper, *Well, I was thinking about it this way. . .*or *I'm not sure I feel right about that. . .* or *I'd like to try to do it this way. . .* but it carries far, gaining power as it goes.

## Different voices

Creating workplaces, organizations, and families that ask people to bring their full measure of self to work requires an honest audit of the range of selves we are prepared to host. Psychologist Carol Gilligan began to uncover the ways that academic research systems had failed to allow for a genuine range of voices while she was teaching at Harvard in the early 1970's. Working as a graduate assistant for psychologists Erik Erikson, a ground-breaking thinker on the development of identity, and Lawrence Kohlberg, a pioneer in the science of moral development, Gilligan began to notice that the young women she was studying didn't fit the categories Erikson and Kohlberg had developed.

Gilligan was particularly interested in the way the women in her studies differed in their approach to moral dilemmas from the men in Kohlberg's work. The content of their responses was different, but even more interesting to Gilligan, and harder to assess with the traditional tools of scientific method, was the way they used—or failed to use—their voices.

Written at the epicenter of feminism, the great tsunami of our times—when large numbers of women were entering into professional, political, and academic arenas—Gilligan's work was revolutionary. When her book, *In a Different Voice: Psychological Theory and Women's Development,* came out in 1982, it called for a complete recalibration of the study of human behavior. Since then it has sold close to a million copies in multiple languages; thousands of dissertations have been derived from it; books have been written about it and more books have been written about those books. It's a song everyone gets now. Sort of.

Despite tectonic shifts in the ways that every field has had to reconsider its assumptions in order to accommodate women's ways of knowing, Gilligan feels the most significant aspect of her breakthrough work has gone untapped. For her, more than any issue of gender, her studies reveal enormous gaps in all of our ability to speak and hear in our real voices.

In overlooking the power of voice as a measure of and source for ways of knowing and transforming ourselves and others, we are not only overlooking women, we are reducing reality. If, as Gilligan proposes, voice is the mother lode for human growth and social transformation and we can't buy it or teach it, both businesses and universities must address themselves better to the task of understanding it.

## Joe McCarthy on finding real voice as a brand

The value of idea-driven businesses will largely be determined by the uniqueness, style, and power of real voice, and their ability to access and cultivate it throughout the organization. The independent visions of great business creators, Stephen Jobs of Apple, Yvonne Chanard of Patagonia, Jeff Bezos of Amazon.com, and Ralph Lauren of Polo are rich with voice. Each one has a *signature* voice, as does every vibrant person we know, be she a musician, CEO, physician, teacher, manager, parent, or friend. A real voice cuts through the fog of bureaucratic language in a way no other force can.

Advertising often seems like annoying clutter. Numbing words awash in a sea of sameness: *Buy me, fly me, try me please or else I'll badger you everywhere—don't think you can escape, I know where you live!* But at its best, advertising is the business of discovering voice.

Every once in awhile, a real voice breaks through; it's just different. A product or company moves you in a gripping, emotional way. Nike is an organization that seems to break through more often than most. To understand the connection between finding voice as an individual, as difficult as that can be, and finding voice as an organization, we went to Joe McCarthy who steered the global advertising division of Nike during the mid nineties when it redefined the depth and reach of brand voice for the rest of business.

You may remember some of the work from Nike's team a black and white documentary montage of girls saying:

> If you let me play sports, I will like myself more. If you let me play, I will be more self-confident. If you let me play, I will be 60% less likely to get breast cancer, I will suffer less depression. If you let me play sports, I will be more likely to leave a man who beats me. If you let me play, I will be less likely to get pregnant before I want to. I will learn what it means to be strong, if you let me play sports.

Or watching, Ric Muñoz as he runs through a park in Los Angeles:

> 80 miles every week. 10 marathons every year. HIV positive.

At a time when violence against women was only beginning to be linked to societal factors, and gay athletes and HIV were still in the closet, Nike told the truth about investment and courage—and told it in a compelling and unsentimental way. When you get it right, it reverberates for years.

## The soul of the brand

McCarthy gave us his best clues for discerning and developing brand with voice:

1. **Find the soul**. The essence of the brand that goes beyond its physical look and the target market is its soul. Soul even goes beyond the heart and the emotional connection. You just *know* when people or things have soul. It's the difference between Marvin Gaye and Michael Bolton.

2. **Be true to your core values.** The spirit of Nike is performance and authenticity. The spirit of Johnson & Johnson is trust and confidence. Unless marketers fully understand the core values of their brand as the basis for all decisions about the brand, they have no true north to guide them in making communication decisions.

3. **Emotion is differentiating**. Understand the set of values and emotions people want to tap into. One of the elements that makes Nike powerful is their understanding of the emotion inherent in all sports, coupled with the distinct emotional dynamics of each sport.

4. **Be Authentic.** Consumers, across the board, can sense what is phony and contrived, and are on the lookout for fakeness. They don't connect with brands that are disingenuous.

## *Building resonant chambers*

Real voice is not particularly loud. A pushy voice with a sharp edge is usually just as false as the whiny voice or the one that constantly apologizes for itself. All of these voices emanate from a shallower place than real voice. The distinction between real and false voices goes beyond motive or the place from which it begins; however, we can hear real voice in its impact on our ears—its timbre, resonance, distinctiveness, and authenticity.

Walk into any organization today, and it's easy to see where the chips are stacked. You see the office stars, the handful of people generating all of the ideas, clout, energy and drive. They know where they're going and the company lives off their firepower. But the rest of the office, the half-spirits, seem to become more listless and disengaged every time a full-spirit walks by. What an inefficient exchange of human resources!

How do we get the spirits on our team to become more real? How do we get every member of our team working as if it mattered? Sometimes they need more direction, more education, more incentives, better equipment, or more support, but the primary things that keep any of us from playing like stars are more internal. They are things like balance, energy, stamina, grace, and confidence, and the sense that we have something to bring to the conversation—and that when we bring it, we will be heard.

## Resonance

*The quality of a cello's sound is formed at the intersection of a player's skill and the resonance of the inner chamber of the instrument itself. An organization has the capacity to serve as a resonant cello chamber for its people, enhancing or diminishing their force and beauty by the resonance with which we surround them.*

This "inner cello world or resonating chamber,"[2] is the defining discovery of Gilligan's recent work on voice. The people around us create an atmosphere that either encourages or distorts our capacity to give voice to our ideas. Keeping a chamber resonant requires mindfulness on everyone's part. It takes a long time to build, and can collapse in a moment.

We build resonance into our communities by speaking in our own real voices. It feels risky, especially because we know how easy it is to hit a wrong note—the clerk who's too perky, the boss who's too folksy, or the manager who's whiny. We're afraid we'll sound like them and it shuts us down. BUT, you do not sound like them! We have to trust our colleagues to recognize our real voices. Building a resonant chamber means having confidence in both the speakers and the listeners within our organizations.

It also means asking second-layer questions. Gilligan has observed that people answer questions according to the level at which it is asked. They may answer a question one way the first time they are asked, and a completely different way the second time, even when the only variable is that they are being asked a second time.

For instance, a colleague tells you he cannot work with one of the managers in your office any longer because the guy's office is a mess and he can't bear walking by it. You listen, then say, "The mess really bugs you doesn't it? Is there anything else about it that gets to you?" He doubles back, "Actually, I don't mind the mess so much as I do the fact that he's always on the phone. He never even looks up to say hello when I walk by."

He's moved from a problem with the guy's messy office to his inattentiveness. A whole other dimension. They are related, but his second issue doesn't deny or expand on the first. Rather, the fact that you've listened longer and asked for more creates a new space, a less urgent and more expectant sounding board. What your colleague is saying is that the manager has made him feel less important than the business of his own desk. Before he says this

**Being heard is the act of being transformed.**

to you, he may actually think the messy office is the problem. In asking him to say more you've asked him to think more, and to think in ways that resonate more deeply.

Because we live and talk at such multiple levels of meaning, sometimes all it takes to move one another to a different level is to ask again. And to know that the second answer doesn't give lie to the first, but acknowledges the multiplicity of our layered relationships to one another. Often we can establish a real voice relationship just by asking, *Can you help me understand this? Is there something I'm not getting? What would you do if the decision were yours to make?*

Listening is the act of gathering; being heard is the act of being transformed. Everyone likes to be listened to; we fear—and long—to be heard. When we know we will be heard, we become smarter, truer, and more fully alive.

## Listening to the counterpoint

*More than listening to the melody, choosing to pay attention to the counterpoint allows us to hear, not only the words of other groups and cultures, but the vast ineffable echoes of history and longing they bring with them. Welcoming them into our inner sanctum of true hearing, the place where we choose our reality.*

If voice is the active choice to make one's mark upon the world, hearing is the choice to be marked by the voices of others. In many ways, we cannot avoid being affected by the voices of those around us. Sometimes they have a weathering or toughening effect on us that can actually dull our hearing, as when we are in a foreign country and become inured to the flow of language around us. After the initial shock—*they really do speak Portuguese in Portugal!*—we don't expect to understand anything.

When we hear other cultures only as one hears traffic or weather; we separate ourselves from it. We do the same thing when we find ourselves in situations we have no context for or expect to have no impact upon. We develop a sort of cultural autism. We can hear the sounds, but we can't imagine they have anything to do with us—or us with them so we tune them out. The alternative is to learn how to hear them.

## Choosing to hear across cultures

In America we talk about *speaking* another language; in Kenya, they talk about *hearing* another language. The educated Kenyan will speak a  ast three languages: English, Swahili, and his own tribal language, but will be able to "hear" a variety of other tribal languages depending on where he grew up and where he has worked and gone to school. Maya Angelou, who has lived in Ghana and Europe, writes about the way that simply hearing another language stretches our capacity to conceive another way of being:

> The American, living in this vast country and able to traverse three thousand miles east to west using the same language, needs to hear languages as they collide in Europe, Africa, and Asia.[3]

Angelou speaks seven languages fluently. She has an ear for several others. As she travels and talks with people across the world, she is always rolling the expressions and music of the languages she hears back into her own. She's currently working on a project in which she's writing children's stories for fifty different cultures—in their own languages.

When asked how she does it, she says, "I try. I learn them because I intend to. If I watch TV, I watch it in Spanish; I choose books to read in French. All of us can learn so much more than we realize. I choose to learn languages because I want to know people."

## When we listen harder

Intentionality, curiosity, and risk-taking are essential to hearing another language, another culture, or another person. Over the last few years I've consciously become more active about *hearing* other cultures. What I'm realizing, of course, is how much I never heard, because I never thought it was about me.

In 1999 my physician husband and I returned to Kenya with our four teenage children for a six-month stint in a rural hospital. Not long after we arrived, we began caring for two orphans, Bui, whose mother had died in childbirth, and Joe, who had been found at three days old in a Nairobi marketplace—not an uncommon phenomenon on a continent where AIDS has orphaned 20 million children.

Through an amazing constellation of good will and good luck, we were able to adopt Bui and Joe, and to bring them back to America as our daughter and son. As you can imagine, the immediate reverberations for our household were significant. The dining room became Bui's bedroom, the kitchen was crowded with highchairs and bottles, and we're still finding old pacifiers under cushions.

For several months, issues of sleep and food overshadowed all else, but eventually larger issues began to make themselves known. We knew we were bringing Joe and Bui to our country, but we began to realize they would be taking us to a new country as well.

We recently heard Dr. Angelou speak at a wedding celebration. She said, "When we marry, we do not do so as individuals—we marry histories." Sometime during the chaotic first year of Joe and Bui's arrival, it struck us in adopting African children into a white American family, we had married histories. Our children, grandchildren, and great-grandchildren would grow up African-American in a world still skewed toward white privilege. If we expected them to grow up gracefully in such a world, the rest of our family needed to learn how to live gracefully in a black world.

> **When we marry, we do not do so as individuals— we marry histories.**

We looked around and realized how little we knew. Our books, our classrooms, our neighborhood, and our church were mostly white. I couldn't even find hair products for Bui at my local pharmacy. We began to make changes wherever we could. We subscribed to *Oprah* and *Jet*, as well as *Time* and *Good Housekeeping*. We began visiting black churches, where we heard about black events and black speakers.

We had always known black individuals, but this was different. For the first time we were coming to know black people in a black context. We were beginning to hear history, politics, religion, and economics in a way we had never heard it before, and we began to realize how much we had missed.

In writing this now, I take the risk of getting it wrong, and by the time you read it, I hope I'm hearing the African-American world better. But some of the lessons I'm learning are:

1. The goodwill extended toward a genuine learner is reward enough for the learner to continue listening.

2. We don't really begin to understand our own language until we begin to learn another one. What's more, our inability to read against the grain of our own culture renders us less intellectually effective in multiple fields.

3. If my beautiful five-year old brown-eyed Joe makes half the mistakes my three blue-eyed teen-age sons have made, he won't get away with it. And when he gets caught or tripped or tricked into whatever trouble a teenage boy is heir to, he will need a deep history of African-American faith, as well as the daily nourishment of his own faith, to bring him through the deadly dangers and temptations of racial discrimination.

**The goodwill extended toward a genuine learner is reward enough for the learner to continue listening.**

Despite our bumper to bumper lives, we all miss hearing each other more often than not. I am making my own *lurch and learn* journey toward hearing a culture better. In making it, I've discovered a growing undercurrent of others who are suddenly aware of conversations they've missed all their lives—*Where was I when all this started? Why didn't I ever hear about this in school? Have we known about this for a long time?* We are hearing whole worlds of ideas for the first time, because we've chosen to. At the heart of our national cynicism about politically correct behavior and multicultural training are two issues:

**A problem of delivery.** Long before many of us had chosen to hear the real questions of cultural inequities, we have already been taught the answers. There is an over-abundance of supply-side political correctness, and too little hunger for trans-cultural understanding. Supply extinguishes demand. No curriculum or training workshop can substitute for the power of choice or hunger to know. We can all increase our own hunger for understanding—as well as the hunger of others, through independent and contagious acts of cross-cultural listening.

**And a problem of conception.** We protect ourselves from the work of learning real cultural theory by playing the "I" card, which protests: *Everyone is an individual and when we talk about gender, race, or culture we reduce individuals to types.* A comforting point of view, but it simply doesn't hold water. The truth is that as we learn more about the values and stories of cultures, we are more able to hear the individuals within them. We don't just hear individuals, we hear histories. Being able to imagine those histories, both as like and unlike our own, is the first unsettling step towards hearing them.

## Choosing to hear across organizations

Research makes it clear that as business leaders move up the food chain, they change cultures and begin to speak a different language. They often lose their ability to hear, not just the feedback, but the real voices, longings, and languages that surround the actual work and exchange they are leading.

A CEO knows his company's vision statement, but he can't hear the roar of frustration and misfires that wash it out at the cash register. This hearing loss runs laterally too. What if the faculty of a university could hear the daily challenges of the admissions department? What if human resources knew what the new business division knows? What if management knew what maintenance knows? The often uncounted cost of power is the loss of easy access to hearing what we need to know.

## Hearing the bad news

The ways in which leaders have failed to hear bad news are epic—from George Custer to Arthur Anderson. Obviously all of us need to develop regular habits and trusted channels for hearing the things we don't want to know. Is my vision clear? Is my ego in check? Am I being distracted by non-essentials? Are my personal wounds undermining my leadership? Am I missing danger signals? Am I stepping on someone's baby? Am I delivering on my promises?

There is always bad news to be had, and little wonder we don't want to hear it. We will always disappoint some people. Both leaders and those they lead are caught in the gap between all of our hopes for a perfect leader and the flesh and blood real one we end up with. Together we must arrive at a continually renewable definition of "a good enough leader."[4] As we learn to hear and give bad news as a part of the ongoing management of our own inevitable shortcomings and disappointments, the exchange becomes less toxic, more normal. Both sides of the management axis can take part in the process of creating a "good enough leader."

## . . . and the good

The value of learning to hear good news across levels of authority and divisions of responsibility, however, is as important as hearing the bad news. And it is hard to hear it across increasingly compartmentalized workplaces in the knowledge economy and the increasingly segmented society outside the workplace. To a great extent, contemporary society has traded in the shackles of patriarchal authority for the new tyranny of sibling rivalry.[5] We no longer listen to the same music, wear the same clothes, or go to the same movies as one another. The downside of this is that a twenty-four year-old man may be speaking to the same problem that his forty-six year-old colleague is working on, but they are unable to draw on one another's draft because they don't realize they're going the same way.

Real hearing inevitably leads to change. And change is unsettling. But it is only through the work of unsettling that we ultimately make room for growth.

Unless we choose to do otherwise, we all miss so much more than we hear. However, when the speakers are brave, the chamber is resonant, and the melodies are rich and diverse, the cycle of hearing and speaking can be marvelously verdant—beyond anything we can grow in silence.

**9**

# SKETCHPAD

*Take the blue pill and stay where you are,*
*take the red pill and see just how deep the rabbit*
*hole goes.*

–Morpheus, *The Matrix*

Sketchpad is the process of getting to our most potent ideas. Focusing on developing ideas as work-in-progress rather than final form and outcome, the sketchpad process encourages us to cycle ideas rapidly and explore their furthest reaches without losing momentum. It requires intuition, resourcefulness, experimentation, curiosity, courage, and collaboration. The role of leadership is to create a nurturing environment and culture that embraces risk, values speed, supports creative problem solving, and encourages people to work openly and cooperatively with raw, unfiltered ideas.

## This is not brainstorming

Have you ever wondered what happens to all the ideas that get generated in brainstorming sessions? Where do those ideas go? Management takes the team off-site, brings in consultants, lets the team members vote for the ideas they like, and then sends everyone back to work. One of our all time favorites, *Tuna in a Tube*, was the number one idea coming out of a recent brainstorming session we attended.

Brainstorming has become a caricature of itself. What began as a promising way to jumpstart the system has lost its spark. We need a less contrived process that works the way people work, not outside the system, but in the core of an organization. We need a way of both generating ideas and working them out continually, whether we are alone in our office, sitting in the hallway with a couple of colleagues, around a board table, or over coffee at Starbucks.

Sketchpad is a way at getting at possibility, form, and direction quickly. In an advertising agency it is the early rapid-fire collaboration of writers and art directors working their ideas, literally sketching them out as they go. For the writer it is following hunches, veins, and interesting paths. It's writing fast, not looking up too soon, and not trying to pin anything down. For the sculptor or photographer, it is a series of figure studies. For the architect, it is flowing reams of concept drawings. For the filmmaker, it is conceiving scenes, rewriting scripts, and shooting early test shots.

## Given permission . . .

More important than the medium of sketchpad is the mindset. Learning how to get to the full force, power, and intuition behind our ideas. Trusting our own vision and instincts while at the same time staying open to other people's input. It's about collaborating while guiding an idea forward. It's accepting we can never know what is going to emerge, but trusting that the creative process will get us through.

More weight-bearing than brainstorming, sketchpad asks us to do more than theorize. It asks us to invent and connect. We must draw the mountain and find the path around it—but we work in pencil, giving us room to double back and try another path if the first one doesn't get there. And no points are taken off for a second try.

The power of sketchpad is that it allows all of us to develop a creative persistence. Not dogged determination, pushing someone else's ideas up an old mountain road with deep ruts, but the fresh, hopeful persistence that comes from working hard with the real expectation of getting to the top.

In our current economy we cannot afford to carry anyone along or to lead him by the hand. Everyone in an organization needs to understand its challenges—and needs to carry his own fuel. By asking for this ongoing work of envisioning and stretching, sketchpad becomes a replenisher of fuel as well as a tool for guidance.

The sketchpad process thrives on limited resources and short deadlines. There certainly is no shortage of *limits* and *lack of* these days. And it is not coincidental that much of our inventive art, music, theater, and film is born in poverty, apart from the wealth of the resources of Broadway

> **The sketchpad process thrives on limited resources and short deadlines.**

and Hollywood. Conception, carrying to term, and the birth of an original idea require indefatigable resourcefulness, imagination, and stretch. Less is more. There is no place for preciousness in the wild. Writing scholar Peter Elbow has long argued for a methodology of hope in the creative process. He says, "I believe that anyone can write with power and eloquence given an occasion of urgency and permission to do so."[1]

Why don't we see more of this kind of innovation in the corporation? Because urgency is masked by cut-and-paste solutions and there is no one willing to give permission. Like the world of advertising, most professions are filled with big-budget, flabby clutter. Remarkably average work, dressed up with bells and whistles, special effects, and slick production values, takes the place of real ideas, the kind of ideas that break through to move us and take us all to a new and better place.

## Sketchpad is dangerous

Working in sketchpad form is quite dangerous in most companies. It requires people to work quickly, cut across lines, share incomplete raw ideas, experiment openly, and try new things. They must be willing to ask questions they don't know the answer to, look less than smart, and be open to building on the ideas of others. Those who really wish to contribute and innovate are perpetually exposed and vulnerable. They become easy targets from almost any direction. You know the rest of the story.

We've seen it from the Ivy League to Madison Avenue. Over and over again we've watched professors and companies reward people for looking smart, playing the angle, staying in control, picking their spots, and presenting their ideas in neat folders with a customized PowerPoint. At the same time, we saw those who displayed true raw brilliance and originality get the crap beat out of them. The system itself has been bankrupting the creative potential of its institutions. Everybody knows the scam and what it costs, but few leaders are brave enough to reverse the suffocating cycle of self-promotion, self-protection, and playing it safe.

## A sustainable growth environment

The kind of environment and management practices we need combine challenge and coaching, stretch and support, freedom and guidance, discovery and comfort, individuals and teams.

It requires knowing our people well—their skills, passions, interests—and asking them to climb the right mountains for themselves and the organization. It provides just enough resources to evoke the fullest range of stretch and challenge without breaking them. It provides feedback not only at review time, but continuously, like a coach with a keen eye for the distinctions that might make the difference in performance. It involves granting the freedom to move through and beyond the organizational structure without hall passes, permission slips, or CYA E-mails.

It's about teams with diverse skills and real individual voice and creating a culture that values discovery, innovation, and creativity.

Elbow believes most of our mistakes come from listening to the critic on our shoulder, whether a shaming boss, a relentless coach, or an angry parent. In moments of urgency we hear their echoes louder than our own good sense, and we pull up short just when we should go long. To write or think or innovate with real power, we need to access the competing muscles of creativity and criticism. Any student of human nature knows that criticism is easier to store, carry, and reproduce than encouragement. Like kudzu, it can take over an environment and choke out the creativity.

In order to create well, we need *hope* in larger doses than *doubt*, and we need to take them early in the process. We need external environments and inner attitudes that allow us to turn off the English teacher and the football coach, until we need them for final editing or resolve. As Elbow puts it, "Both believing and doubting should get their half of the bed."[2]

## Take a full swing

Actress/director/writer Joan Darling is no newcomer to the sketchpad process. Her capacity and speed for making daring associations, along with her sense of humor and her insight into the human predicament, have had a palpable effect on the shape of the American entertainment industry. With a shrewd eye and uncanny ear, Emmy-recipient Darling has given us some of the funniest moments in TV history, directing ground-breaking episodes of shows like *MASH, Taxi, Rhoda, The Mary Tyler Moore Show* and *Mary Hartman, Mary Hartman*. Remember Sally and Morrie on *The Dick van Dyke Show*? Remember when Chuckles the Clown bit the dust on *The Mary Tyler Moore* show? That was Darling.

To watch Joan Darling at work at the Sundance Institute, or in Chapel Hill where she is a professor at the University of North Carolina, is to see her exercising her genius as a midwife to the creative process for both actors and writers. Her students know intuitively that Darling is not looking for their best practice swing, but the real thing. "To get people to take a full swing, you need to educate them, love them and seduce them into it. They need to allow themselves to go all the way to the end of their skulls in their own imagination." With twinkling eyes and contagious pleasure in the process, Darling is a sort of Mother Theresa with attitude, welcoming her students' whiffs and their home runs, and helping them discover the best in their ideas.

**We spend too much time marking and measuring with our putter when we're still 400 yards from the green.**

We spend too much time marking and measuring with our putter when we're still 400 yards from the green. If we get the weight of our imagination behind a good drive and follow it all the way through, we'll often end up remarkably close to the pin. We'll be closer to the center of a great idea, and able to see a better picture of what we want to do and get a clearer sense of how to get there. Taking a big swing at an idea heightens our natural sense of aim.

Fears and perfectionism hold us back from finding our best ideas. Darling compares the creative process to topiary pruning. . . "Perfectionism applied too soon also kills creativity. You need to allow the bush to grow in an oddly messy way. A perfectionist, who doesn't trust the ultimate cohesion that will come about, will cut too soon before the growth has fully come alive."

### Chaos is scary and tomorrow keeps coming

Chaos is the essential source of all real growth. The first step in creation is to generate chaos, then to form or compose it. Until we learn to face chaos, we're not growing anything, we're simply re-arranging the cushions on a ship in dry dock.

Children have the unique capacity to both explore chaos and to order it. They run down a steep path without knowing where it's leading or if anyone has been down it before. Maps, handrails, knee braces, and fear of falling come later—good, preservational things to have as we grow older. But to truly create we need to protect the exercise of faith and hope as well as our energy and our knees.

For innovative organizations, too many guardrails may diminish the courage it takes to face the resource of genuine chaos. Twenty-five years ago when Bill Hybels began to sketch a vision for a different kind of church, Nancy Beach was a teenager in his youth group and joined in his search for new ways to deliver old truths. Since that time, Beach has been a chief architect behind a new concept of worship that has reshaped the way church services are being done throughout the world today. She has brought drama, contemporary music, multi-media, story, and choreography to a field that had been organized around an organ, two hymns, and a choir number for hundreds of years.

After twenty years of stunning success at her work, Beach's team has influenced thousands of churches worldwide who have attended their "Worship and the Arts" conferences and are using their materials. What is her greatest challenge? Keeping it fresh.

Why doesn't Beach take a rest? Why doesn't she recycle some of the creative material her group has generously disseminated to so many other churches? Because in xeroxing the product, they would lose the process. Her team is vastly bigger, their calendar is more extended, and her resources are more complex than when she began, but each Tuesday morning as Beach meets with the team who is planning a Sunday's worship, they start with a blank page. They face the power of chaos, and they sketch boldly.

As we grow older, if we don't take care to stretch our imaginative muscles, we find ourselves halting and clutching for footholds; we tend to look down too often, and we lose our range.

An athlete loses his flexibility with age unless he continues to stretch and stay supple. Unless it takes great care to do otherwise, the human mind has the same tendency and so does the human organization.

## 10 ideas for working the Sketchpad Process

1. To improve aim, take full swings, not precise measurements.
2. Check your baggage at the door. Fear, negativity, preconceived outcomes are killers.
3. Be visual. Keep creating simple mental pictures, sketches, and concept drawings.
4. Stay focused on developing the idea. Resist the temptation to dress it up and hide it behind bells and whistles.
5. Allow the idea to happen and fully emerge. Certainty, exactness, and efficiency come later and are detrimental if applied too soon.
6. Improvise the resources you do not have. Build the imaginative eye.
7. Switch roles. Occasionally have art directors write and writers direct art. It will open up new synapses, understanding, and perspective.
8. Keep looking at the idea through multiple lenses. Engage others in the collaboration to further work the ideas, let them build on it.
9. Keep track of what's working and what's not. As you push deeper into the forest of unfamiliar territory, this information will be your guideposts to help you when you get lost.
10. Stay open to the ideas of others, but do not lose sense of your own vision.

## 10

# SPACE

*We shape our dwellings, thereafter, our dwellings shape us.*

–Winston Churchill

Space. It requires an architecture that facilitates information and energy, allowing the full scope of our knowledge to flow in and through it. It is a resource of stimulation, inspiration, and communication. The role of leadership is to conceive, design and utilize space in a way that enhances planned and spontaneous interactions while connecting disciplines of knowledge. In music or design, we talk about *dead* space, space that doesn't conduct energy or manage its reverberations. We're speaking here of the quintessentially *live* space of communication—space that becomes a generative source of ideas.

## Re-Thinking space

When we redefine space, it becomes clear that architecture, environment, and atmosphere are unexplored frontiers for organizations that are serious about sustainable growth. Space, the place(s) where we conceive and cultivate, is critical for organizational innovation. It works for us or against us. But re-arranging the furniture or jumping on the latest design fad misses the point. For great work in the Age of Ideas, a new kind of architecture is needed.

In today's world of architecture, breathtaking expressionist sculptures and cubist abstractionist buildings dominate the headlines. Spectacular signature buildings may serve well as museums and tourist attractions, but the more time we spend inside these heroic spaces, the more limiting and inflexible they feel.

The work of Frank Lloyd Wright is stunningly cohered. Everything in it relates to everything else in it with unity and exacting precision that is arresting to look at, but can be restrictive to live in. It lacks today's freedom of eclecticism: the juxtaposition of rich combinations of diverse things in the same space. As we learned from architect Robert Venturi, "Wright designed the andirons, the chairs, virtually everything in the house. He ultimately tried to design even the frocks of the women who would inhabit his houses."[1] A chair designed by Frank Lloyd Wright looks great, but you might not choose it to sit in at the end of a long day.

## Beyond form and function

Form or function? For too long, discussions about art and architecture have centered on this binary. But the Age of Ideas calls for spaces that push beyond both considerations, for spaces that work at a more complex level than mere aesthetics or practicality. These spaces will function not as something you look at, the medieval tapestry on the wall, or as something you use, the oriental carpet on the floor, but as both. What's more it will require a third element. Because the world's economies have become more complex, interconnected, and faster, new creative spaces will have to conduct an ongoing exchange of energy and information. A new architecture of exchange must emerge.

I first started thinking differently about space when I was desperately looking for growth for my North Carolina advertising firm. My thoughts were triggered by an interview I gave for *Bloomberg News* at their New York headquarters. Bloomberg was pioneering 24/7/365 news delivery and the energy that reverberated around their studios was electric.

The hub seemed to be the café, where they were serving breakfast, lunch, and dinner all at the same time. At any given moment, someone would be starting his day, and at the same time, another person would be eight hours into it. The café was a hot bed of idea exchange, information hand-offs, and stimulation—a kind of wild, unpredictable, cross-pollinated garden of ideas.

This was at the beginning of the Internet boom, and I became fascinated by the human element of how we could orient a workforce as well as ourselves to an emerging around the clock world of continuous information flows and opportunities. Later at LHC, I brought George Stephanopoulos to North Carolina to describe the creation of the Clinton campaign's War Room, a unique space that allowed them to work in real time and to quickly connect diverse and divergent sources.

**What kind of atmosphere, environment, and space fosters continuous innovation?**

I wanted to understand where the leading idea companies got their ideas. What kind of atmosphere, environment, and space fosters continuous innovation?

### From dentist office to war room

While at Long Haymes Carr, I began to experiment with the development of live space for corporate work. This was no small challenge given that we started out with what one client described as a 1970's dental office.

We built a 24/7 café and offered free, healthy food, and beverages. We took down doors, walls, and barriers of every type, creating as much community space as possible. We built a wall of inspiration with rows of open shelves in our entryway where people could leave artifacts for others to see and take if inspired to do so. We gave people buckets of paint, furniture allowances and total freedom to create individual workspaces that would best enable them to find their voice.

We commissioned installation artist Stephen Hendee, whose work we first experienced at P.S.1 Contemporary Art Center, New York's celebrated alternative museum, to transform a sterile conference room into a kind of cathedral of inspiration. The moment you entered the space it produced a change in both mind and body, calming and stimulating at the same time, like the feeling of looking at stained glass windows in a cathedral. This is exactly the frame of mind needed for sketchpad thinking and creative problem solving.[2]

We experimented with a four-day work week, organizing ourselves to work more efficiently in order to leave Fridays open for symposium in our atrium with the entire agency staff, our clients, and community members. We filmed these sessions and sent out highlights on the web to every member of our growing community. The topics ranged from Chaos Theory Physics, to Marketing Aesthetics, to the Digital Revolution.

Although we initially encountered some resistance to these ideas, people gradually started to feel the strength of discovery as they accessed an expanding network of resources across a variety of fields. It was a dynamic and nurturing environment that resulted in output from the staff that improved daily.

That immediate success at LHC gave us a clue to the infinite possibilities latent in space. If we could only conceive it in new ways. As a part of the *Odyssey Project,* I began to seek out fertile environments, as well as new platforms within environments, for generating energy, fostering unlikely connections, and facilitating dynamic flows of information and ideas. We were looking for an architecture born, not from Newtonian action-reaction concept of space and time, but from something more. We were looking for an architecture that could maximize the rich cultural variety of *now,* one that could facilitate the organization's need to deal with speed, complexity, and change, and that could become part of the sustainable competitive advantage for an organization.

I began my quest by investigating how some of the world's great information and idea companies were conceiving and using space. I was led to Palo Alto to collaborate with IDEO, the legendary design firm that brought the world the Apple mouse, the Palm handheld, and the Polaroid I-Zone instant camera. My quest also led me to Imagination in London, one of the world's finest environmental design/brand experience companies, and a driving force behind the creation of the Guinness Storehouse in Dublin. In these spaces, you feel the movement of ideas and energy as clearly as the mist on your face as you walk through a rainforest. This is the atmosphere that liberates creativity.

At IDEO and Imagination, the energy flows are vibrant, but not frenetic. Structurally, physical barriers are minimal. Sight lines are open, movement is visible, and visual perspectives are varied. There are multiple paths for getting around, and there are common spaces where both formal and informal gatherings are encouraged. There are spaces to get loud and individual spaces for quiet thinking and reflection. The sources of stimuli are abundant—unusual periodicals, cable feeds, and personal totems from individual and collective discoveries.

**You can feel the movement of ideas and energy as clearly as the mist on your face as you walk through a rainforest.**

Artifacts and ideas are catalogued so as to be accessed by all and randomly scattered, to enable chance discovery. There are spaces designed for continual change, similar to a lab or a theater set. There are communication tools of every conceivable type to facilitate collaboration both inside the organization and with the outside world. The architecture supports a continuous and unpredictable process of discovery. The environment facilitates a framework that mixes disciplines, talents, information flows, and idea exchange and encourages a kind of messy experimentation, a continuous collision of unlikely ideas and people connecting in planned and unforeseen ways, and a design of ongoing vigilance for breaking down bunkers and silos of knowledge.

## *Learning from Las Vegas*

Our search to find clear, advanced thinking about architecture that fostered live space communication led us to Philadelphia, the home of architects Robert Venturi and Denise Scott Brown. Venturi, a recipient of architecture's coveted Pritzker Prize, and his partner/wife, Scott Brown, are revered by academe and this generation's rising architectural stars, many of whom point to them as mentors. Although their names are little recognized by the business world, New Yorker columnist Paul Goldberger writes, "Just as Freud and Einstein made it impossible to look at their fields in the same way again, Venturi and Brown have changed the way we see the world."[3]

As early as the 1960s, Venturi and Scott Brown saw powerful forces changing the American landscape and anticipated their 21st century manifestations long before anyone else. Their sources of inspiration are eclectic, far-reaching, and unexpected. For instance, their first breakthrough insights into the architecture of exchange began in the desert...in Las Vegas...on the strip...in a car...at 35mph! It was in the fall of 1968, Scott Brown and Venturi had led a scouting team to study the Las Vegas strip. Says Venturi in a confident, commanding, mellifluous, John Chancellor-like tone,

The movement from architecture as space to architecture as communication has only just begun to happen. There's a lot of precedent for it. The Egyptian hieroglyphs on the ancient pylons, the murals all over Italian churches, mosaics looking like electronic pixels in Byzantine and early Christian churches, where you are being informed. These churches are essentially billboards, informing, teaching, and you can even say selling religious theology to the populous, who were, by the way, mostly illiterate.

There's an irony in the fact that we have the same thing today, pixilated surfaces, but because it's electronic we can make it moving information. Our content can be changing all the time, and we can connect to a multicultural age where there are lots of kinds of information that have to go out. It's not a monoculture any more. Times Square today is the equivalent of the Piazza San Marco in Venice, the great ribbon complex.

Venturi and Scott Brown have developed this vision into an iconographic architecture, alive with electronics, signage, LED, lasers, aesthetic pixels, and digital images.[4] They envisioned buildings as dynamic electronic shelters with exteriors of glittering information with increasing speed and expanding scale, pulsing rhythmically, organic and alive, vital and content-rich, all moving in real time. These ideas have shaped the thinking of contemporary architecture, and ultimately led to the kind of buildings that are now appearing in Times Square—the NASDAQ, Viacom, and Morgan Stanley buildings. Theirs is an architecture of content, rather than abstraction, a 24-hour architecture for communication for now.

## The architecture of sound

While Venturi and Scott Brown have been redesigning the architecture of physical space, Chris Hardman has spent his life experimenting with the live space of sound. If you've been to the Getty, the Louvre, or the National Air and Space Museum in the last few years, you've encountered his work. Using the simple technology of the *Walkman*, the portable headsets that first individualized music listening twenty years ago, Hardman has transformed the way individuals encounter the world of art. Instead of being shushed and pushed as a group through museums and historic sites while captive to the uninterruptible spiel of tour guides, we can now put on our headsets and listen to the history and details of each aspect of a tour at our own pace. We can linger in front of the *Mona Lisa* and sprint by Picasso, or vice versa. By conceiving and designing customized story telling, Hardman has changed the way that we encounter great visions and voices from the past—one person, one painting, one concept, and one encounter at a time.

Hardman, now the artistic director of Antenna Theater, has put his boldest ideas into this experimental project that seeks to individualize the way we experience live theatre. His goal is to physicalize knowledge:

> We experience the world in ways far beyond just hearing and seeing. We smell it, touch it, move through it, and that movement is a lot of the education of who we are, and who somebody else is. Antenna puts you physically inside someone else's behaviors, as opposed to watching an actor in that role. When you watch, you may empathize, but you don't leap into that skin.

Rather than having a large audience watch a few actors playing out the parts that they've learned, Antenna Theater is designed to give every theater-goer an opportunity to imagine the events of the play as if he were at its center. Attending a theater experience called *Euphorium,* I was fitted with headphones, an MP3 player, and a helmet with a distinctive individual screen, and led through a series of chambers to envision the evening's performance as both actor and audience. I was Samuel Coleridge experiencing the three-hour nap he was taking when he dreamed the vision that became the epic poem *Kubla Kahn.* Instead of watching an actor encountering Abysinnian maidens and sacred rivers, I encountered them myself.

Hardman has tapped into a well of boundless power through simple technology by personalizing the listening experience. He says, "Audio is so fluid, you can easily change a sound environment from echoic and harsh, to intimate and seductive, as well as collage diverse sounds from other sources such as radio and films. In the audio realm,

**Consider the ways we are currently squandering the live spaces of sound.**

we can allow things to just kind of appear and disappear, like thoughts in our minds." Hardman's attention to the ear as well as to the eye taps into what we already know—our ears record emotion and make sense of relationships better than our eyes.

If Hardman can use sound to put a tourist in the center of Celtic England or an audience in the center of Samuel Coleridge's mind, we are surely squardering the influence of sound in the places we work and in the work that we do there.

## Physiological architecture

Our final tour of space led us to San Francisco to encounter Decosters & Rahm breaking new ground with their work in physiological architecture. These Swiss architects operate at the intersection of technology, biology, and space to create "intelligent" environments that influence human physiology. We first experienced their ideas in an exhibition titled *Melatonin Room*[5]. Melatonin is a naturally occurring chemical produced by the body. A high level causes sleepiness, while a low level produces high energy and alertness.

As you enter the first room, a high intensity green light blocks the production of melatonin and you can feel the stimulation and energy. As you enter a second room, the light diminishes in intensity and becomes ultraviolet, thereby increasing the body's production of melatonin, and you feel the calming effect. As we reflect on the bad air and poor lighting in the environments most of us work in today, their ideas seem as revolutionary to us as the modern office of today might seem to a turn-of-the-century textile worker.

## Space, the final frontier

Today's leaders need to get as serious about the architecture of space, sound, and physiology, and its impact on the productivity of the knowledge worker as earlier leaders had to get about factory design and its impact on the productivity of the industrial worker. The management conversation must evolve from paint colors and rug swatches to a full understanding of space. In today's economy, all of our spaces must be live; they must invite and enact exchange; and they must express the ethos of our organizations.

# Conversations
## With
# Mad Dogs, Dreamers and Sages

Part III

# Introduction

*Our duty is to return bearing the gifts of the grail within ourselves, that we might be a cup, a means of regeneration to every living creature.*

–John Matthews

Innovation relies on vision—on seeing untapped value. Today, in the Age of Ideas, when there is so much less surplus available to the material eye—no gold nuggets lying around, no herds of buffalo—our great resources for growth lie beyond the visible. As Plato explained in his concept of the imagination, *it's the thing behind the thing* that is rich with possibility. To see it requires the imaginative eye. And it can be cultivated!

You may have had a place in your childhood where your imaginative eye worked better than usual: in your garage, under your neighbor's porch, up in the attic, down at the creek behind your house. If you were to return to those places today, your material eye might find them surprisingly small, maybe even shabby. Were the friendships, adventures, and stories that you experienced there false or unworthy? Or were they real and vivid, but your imaginative eye has lost its strength? Atrophied? Any artist will tell you that the imaginative eye is a muscle that grows with exercise—and that its magic for childhood is rudimentary compared to its power for adults.

Can you feel it? Absolutely. It is the muscle we stretch when we wake in the middle of a dream and try to get back into it; it's the empathetic problem-solver set into motion by someone else's problem; and it's the resource we too often leave behind when we go to work. Like an old car in the garage, it becomes sluggish not from age, but for want of driving fast on the open road. Imagine a work environment like the one you and your cousins created in your backyard, where the continuum of vision was not arithmetic, but exponential. Some strength of the imagination is developed in our individual Walden Ponds, but history testifies to the clustering of its fruit, from the flowering of symphonic music in nineteenth-century Germany with Brahms and Beethoven to the explosion of technology in the Silicon Valley in the nineties.

**The imaginative eye is a muscle that grows with exercise.**

These clusterings develop because the imaginative vision is contagious. Those who develop it become sources of stimulation, interaction, and excitement. Magnets for learning, commerce and communication. They attract talent and excite an effervescent flow of experimentation. In these heady atmospheres, conventions fall away and new ideas, experiences, and expressions emerge.[1]

### Inklings networks

The recent release of the film *The Return of the King,* leaves one more ripple from the conversations of the Inklings, a group of thinkers, believers and writers who gathered together around C.S. Lewis half a century ago. Lewis, J.R.R. Tolkein, and a small group of friends gathered each Tuesday morning for beer at the Eagle and Child, a small pub in Oxford, England. It was an unlikely group—a linguist, a literary scholar, a doctor, a barrister, and a soldier. They called themselves the Inklings and met for 15 years, a period which included the bleak days of World War II in

England. Their talk was, as Lewis puts it, "red meat and strong beer for the soul."

One of our discoveries in this project was a host of "Inklings networks." Working out of the roots of *Psychology Today*, T George Harris has developed a virtual round table of idea makers and sharers. For decades Harris has met regularly with his own Inklings group. At its core are the regulars—Peter Drucker, Dan Yankelovich and, until his death in 1970, Abraham Maslow, the founder of humanistic psychology. But hundreds of others have stepped in and out of its permeable borders.

In her work on women, Carol Gilligan developed her own group of scholars who pushed the borders of women's studies outward together. In a more formal way, Robert Redford has gathered a growing community of filmmakers and artists interested in pushing the limits of independent film at Sundance. And on an even vaster scale, Willow Creek Community Church has developed a vast network and exchange of resources through the 10,000 member Willow Creek Association which brings artists, youth leaders, pastors, and laity together in conferences all over the world.

We've all benefited from the fruit of these groups, disseminated more widely and generously than we can imagine. Though the aim of this project is to encourage each person to cultivate a roundtable of ideas, we wanted to give you a few glimpses of the mad dogs, dreamers, and sages as we found them—in the midst of their own Inklings around the world. And so we give you our snapshots of the mad dogs, dreamers, and sages.

## Snapshots of the Mad Dogs

What we are offering in this chapter is a scrapbook of snapshots, cuttings from the floor, and the offhand words that have stuck with us for some reason as we've carried the work of the project along. Read it more like an on-the-road journal than an encyclopedia. These are the pictures we caught on a given day and in a specific place.

## Sundance

One of the purest examples of sustained growth, innovation and creative culture is Robert Redford's Sundance Institute. With gracious permission from *Inc.* magazine where we first published our ideas on Sundance, we begin our description of these mad dogs and their communities, with our learning from Sundance.[2]

## 11

# Sundance:
# The Perfect Host for the Age
# Of Ideas

*When you have the good fortune to have success in your life, I've always thought that is precisely the time you should reinvent yourself. You should go right back to zero as though nothing had happened and start again. Because you can get real stale. You can fall in love with yourself or get to that danger point when you could ride on that success or try to repeat it. Repetition makes me very nervous.*

–Robert Redford

Redford has suggested we tour his 6,000-acre complex in Sundance, Utah, on horseback, and that is clearly how these wild western mountains are meant to be viewed. But horses terrify me—always have—and while I yearn to saddle up with the Sundance Kid in a prototypical act of male bonding…I just can't. Redford is nice as can be about it, and soon we are trekking along a footpath leading away from Sundance Village, surrounded by tall pines and wooded canyons. And I am glad we are on foot because it means I can give Redford my full attention as he talks about how it feels to build something from nothing, and how he encourages the people he works with to do that day after day after day.

Fit and rugged in blue jeans and running shoes, Redford points to the rockwork on the village restaurant. "Sweat equity!" he declares. "I did a lot of the work myself. And when you do something by hand—it's just different." The pride in his voice is quintessentially entrepreneurial, which isn't surprising: Redford is the quintessential entrepreneur. The birth legend of Sundance is positively Lincoln-esque: In 1961, the then-24-year-old actor bought two acres of land for $500 and built a log cabin there. Today Sundance is an international enterprise that includes a cable channel, a DVD/video line, a retail catalog, a resort, and—as its nucleus—a not-for-profit institute that is part artists' colony, part R&D shop and that also produces the annual Sundance Film Festival. All of it, says Redford, furthers a single goal: "the sponsoring of a process that will allow people to have new visions and new voices."

> **And when you do something by hand—it's just different.**

If new voices and visions are the "products" of Sundance, they are products whose success most businesspeople would envy. Sundance, after all, is among the very few organizations that can credibly claim to have pioneered a market: the market for independent film, which continues to withstand the hurricane force of Hollywood sequels, event movies, and saturation marketing. Its film and theater labs have helped develop such groundbreaking work as *Raising Victor Vargas, Boys Don't Cry, Reservoir Dogs, Requiem for a Dream, Love & Basketball, Hedwig* and *The Angry Inch, Angels in America, I Am My Own Wife,* and *The Laramie Project.* And Sundance has contributed to the emergence of a constellation of artists that includes Quentin Tarantino, Allison Anders, John Cameron Mitchell, Wes Anderson, Paul Thomas Anderson, Craig Lucas, Tony Kushner, and Julie Taymor.

Nor is the organization doing badly by standards unrelated to art. In a nation where so many projects and products fail, 35% of projects developed in the Sundance Filmmakers Lab and 85% of its Theater Lab projects make it to production—in other words, producers outside Sundance consider them promising enough to finance and complete. That's more than 85 feature films in 22 years. The brand is so well recognized it has become shorthand for independent filmmaking. There's a Sundance shelf in more than 4,000 Blockbuster stores.

Redford has also built commercial enterprises—some of them profitable—that further his goal of creating venues for innovative work. (Sundance does not release revenue figures.) The Sundance Channel, launched in 1996 as a joint venture by Redford, Showtime Networks, and Universal Studios, has grown steadily and now has 16.7 million subscribers, according to Kagan World Media. (The market-leading Independent Film Channel has 26.8 million subscribers.) A documentary channel is on the way, and a new Sundance Film Series is rolling out in 10 major markets this fall. Redford has also speculated about launching an investment arm and even a production company, in essence becoming a full-fledged manufacturer of the products Sundance now develops and markets.

"Redford is a proven, smart, savvy entrepreneur," says Dale Pollock, veteran Hollywood producer and dean of the filmmaking department at North Carolina's School of the Arts. "The business potential is enormous. Sundance has the best brand name and the ability to expand its audience base."

"How large the indie film niche can become, I don't think anyone really knows," says Pollock. "As for profitability, it may not be huge by mainstream Hollywood standards yet. But it's growing significantly, and Sundance is the lead player positioned in the right way."

Such prolificacy is not the consequence of mountain air or movie star charisma. Rather it springs from Redford's unshakable belief that growth is not an accounting practice but a creative process. And that goes not just for the entertainment industry, but also for ordinary companies that make sunscreen and software and ceiling fans. "The more I got involved with business, the more I got shocked at how dumb a lot of businesses were. Even the ones that had so much money," Redford says. "And, it's because they lacked a creative, imaginative approach. That's why I got taken with people like Steve Jobs and [Patagonia founder] Yvon Chouinard and [Smith & Hawken founder] Paul Hawken, who understood exactly how important business is but also understood the role of the creative.

"Do you think the earth was created by an accountant?" Redford asks me. "No! The earth was created by the combustion of a creative explosion. Fire and chaos are what started everything. Then order came on top of that."

It is to study Sundance's own creative explosion that I am here. And while I hate to digress, I think at this point I should say a word about myself and why I believe business can learn so much from Sundance.

First—and let's just get this out of the way—I'm a businessperson, not a journalist. For most of the '90s I was CEO of Long Haymes Carr (LHC), an advertising firm in Winston-Salem, N.C., that in three years grew from the 100th largest U.S. agency to the 50th. One tool we used to differentiate ourselves was Creative Odyssey—a series of magical mystery tours to cities like New York, London, and New Orleans where our clients and employees immersed themselves in the leading edge of pop culture. We met with people like graffiti artists and chaos theory physicists to experience new perspectives. We escorted Fortune 1000 CEOs to hip-hop stores and encouraged them to buy chartreuse sandals with four-inch heels and flame-toed Doc Martens and wear them on the subway. Again and again we found that most of the ideas and strategies for our breakthroughs came from sources outside the business world.

Then one day our corporate parent announced it was consolidating our agency...ultimately out of existence.

Disillusioned and reluctant to return quickly to corporate life, I began looking around the business world for my next opportunity. What I saw wasn't pretty.

This was the fall of 2001, a time when corporate misjudgments and miscreants were ubiquitous on the news. Everywhere companies were slowing down, stopping, shifting into reverse. I saw the artificial growth of acquisitions and book-cooking collapsing everywhere, but no sustainable, organic growth based on the invention of genuinely new markets, products, and services. Where was the real top-line growth, I wondered? Had management forgotten how to do it? Was business losing the ability?

Organic growth, it seemed to me, required something I've come to think of as "imaginative intelligence": the ability to convert the raw material of experience and insight across disciplines of knowledge into inventive work. Having experienced something like that on LHC's Odysseys, I wondered whether others had figured out how to build imaginative intelligence into their processes and organizations. I cashed in my frequent-flier miles and gave myself a year to find out.

Together with my colleague Jane Stephens I launched the Odyssey Project, a wide-ranging exploration of organic growth focused on 30 innovation leaders in diverse fields. Creative Odyssey had taught me the value of seeking answers from nonobvious sources, so I excluded destinations like Intel, Apple, and Southwest Airlines from my itinerary. Instead I traveled to Willow Creek Community Church outside Chicago, which pioneered the idea of growing exclusively through conversion, and Antenna Theater, an experimental stage company in San Francisco that found commercial success creating interpretive audio programs for museums and parks. Rather than try to meet with Peter Drucker or Gary Hamel, I interviewed T George Harris, the maverick editor of *Psychology Today* who broke ground in developing interest-specific journalism, Dan Yankelovich, who reinvented public polling with the Yankelovich Monitor, and the poet Maya Angelou.

Finally I landed here, at Sundance. And in this place most people associate with celebrity and conservation, I discovered the purest example of sustained innovation and creative organizational culture I had yet seen.

The not-for-profit Sundance Institute nurtures creativity in writers and filmmakers; folks you'd think wouldn't need the assist. But you would be wrong. Just consider what those filmmakers were putting out, chiefly under the aegis of Hollywood, before Redford, in true change agent style, forged the marketplace for independent movies. Films like *Sex, Lies and Videotape* may have wedged open the door, but without a constant flow of new—and not just new but exciting—products that door would have closed. For independent film to become a movement, later an industry, artists had to recover their voices, or learn they had them in the first place. It is the same challenge facing engineers, designers, and others who staff R&D efforts in industries and companies suffering from an idea drought.

For more than 20 years the Sundance Institute has churned out original ideas with the regularity of sausage. I wanted to know how it did that. So I spent five days at Sundance, sitting in on workshops with filmmakers, interviewing staff members at length, and talking with successful alumni.

Most important, I listened to Redford.

It is routine, in matters of art, to say the creation mirrors the mind of the creator. Sundance is not a work of art—it is an organization with employees, budgets, and multiple commercial and noncommercial arms—but it mirrors Redford's mind as exactly as if he had dreamed it and then drawn it upon waking. To understand Sundance, therefore, one must first understand Redford. And in getting to know the man, I glimpsed Sundance's first lesson for entrepreneurs: that the key to a constantly innovating organization is a constantly innovating founder.

Redford is always restless, and his appetite for fresh thought is enormous. "When you have the good fortune to have success in your life, I've always thought that is precisely the time you should reinvent yourself. You should go right back to zero as though nothing had happened and start again," says Redford. "Because you can get real stale. You can fall in love with yourself or get to that danger point when you could ride on that success or try to repeat it. Repetition makes me very nervous."

Redford created the Sundance Institute, in part, to combat the deadening repetition that he saw stifling the film industry. But it was his instincts for nurturing creativity in others that has made it thrive.

Like all entrepreneurs, Redford has been guided by a vision. Unlike most, he doesn't compromise it.

That may sound hopelessly unrealistic to most founders, who would argue—reasonably—that for the overwhelming majority of folks who aren't Robert Redford financial and commercial pressures are tough to withstand. But Redford feels those pressures too: "It's been a struggle, and it continues to be a struggle. I've learned a lot of hard lessons," he says. And of course when he began to envision Sundance back in 1966,

**In Sundance, he envisioned an organization that would be a double sanctuary, a creative vortex where art and nature could flourish.**

Redford wasn't Redford either. The young actor built his first log cabin in the Provo Canyon as a kind of sanctuary. As his attachment to the valley grew, Redford worried about the future of the land—threatened by development—and of the industry in which he worked. America's entertainment culture was becoming increasingly impoverished: Redford saw independent film as its best hope. In Sundance, he envisioned an organization that would be a double sanctuary, a creative vortex where art and nature could flourish.

To build such an organization, Redford had to learn about business, which he did the same way he learned everything else—

by observing, guessing, and revising. "I surprised myself early on by growing really fascinated with business," says Redford. "I had bought the land, and I had to make deals with banks, and I had to make payments, and I didn't know what I was doing. I had to learn fast."

"It became like an acting exercise," Redford continues. "I had to act like I was a normal human being. I had to act like I was more conservative than I was. I had to act like I knew about business. It was challenging and fun."

As a business, Sundance got off to a rocky start. The first thing Redford wanted to do was buy land—lots of it. His plan was to start with a resort that would generate enough money to make the loan payments without compromising the area's natural beauty. But when he invited investors out to Provo, all they saw was real estate. Those partners bought the land with him but not the vision. Laughing, Redford speculates what they were thinking: "Redford's out of his mind—he doesn't have a clue about business. As soon as we get into the deal, he'll learn real fast what the story is and he'll submit to real estate [development] right off the bat!" They were wrong. Even with payments looming, Redford refused to sell off subdivisions, and his partners eventually gave in.

If Redford's fellow investors had any doubts about his attitude toward compromise those doubts soon vanished. The partners wanted to build a restaurant next to the ski lift, the obvious spot since it would get the most traffic. "No, no, no," Redford recalls himself saying. "Let's give it its own space, let people wander and discover it." But there was a tree smack in the middle of Redford's proposed site. "Well, that's great!" Redford said. "We'll build it around the tree and call it the Tree Room."

His partners balked. "According to the formula, you'll lose 12 eating-places," they argued. "Then 12 fewer people will eat," Redford responded.

Soon after that, Redford's partners sold their interests, and Redford assumed the whole load in 1970. "They realized I was an impossible partner—and they were right," he says. Redford and three friends built the restaurant by hand for $19,000. There were many problems. The original partners had made a bad deal on the land, "and we bought it from a sheepherder," says Redford. Even the tree died. But Redford planted another tree, and today the Tree Room is profitable and recognized as one of the finest restaurants in the state. "I just believed we could do something incorporating the environment that would make it more meaningful, and they believed you had to put the environment away from it and go straight to business," says Redford.

"You have to think not only revenue, but the quality of that revenue," Redford says. It is a philosophy he has never abandoned.

Under a brilliant blue sky the village of Sundance is framed by conservation land lush with ponderosa pine and quaking aspen. Once an isolated canyon and the sacred hunting and storytelling ground of the Ute tribe, the area remains serenely quiet. The loudest sound is rushing water, still high from the spring runoff from snow-spired Mount Timpanogos.

Sundance's rough-sawn post-and-beam structures include a rehearsal hall, screening room, outdoor amphitheater, general store, the Tree Room restaurant, the Owl Bar, and cottages. Intimate in scale, the buildings are connected by simple paths and footbridges. Their rich natural hues blend easily with the colors of the land.

Not to be confused with the famous Sundance Film Festival held each winter in nearby Park City, the programs of the Sundance Institute are housed chiefly in this village, among the first simple structures Redford built more than 20 years ago. The institute is the engine behind Redford's vision, a carefully tended, highly productive series of experimental labs and mentoring programs offered year-round for emerging and professional directors, screenwriters, playwrights, composers, and theater artists. Individually and together, they are making a stand against formulaic entertainment.

In movies today, "there's a kind of soullessness, a blandness, a homogenization of story, of character in order to attempt to please everyone," says actor-director Stanley Tucci, an institute alumni who spoke to me by phone while filming in New York. Redford puts it this way: "Film viewing is extremely impersonal now; it's almost hostile. You have 40 screens. You usher people in and out as quickly as possible to get in as many [shows] per day [as possible]. The real money is made in the concessions."

Hollywood, in other words, is a Raisinets economy. It was to combat that growing homogenization that Redford established the institute in 1981 as an incubator for raw talent and divergent visions. In the early years, the actor supported the institute out of his own personal wealth. Today 35% of its $15 million budget comes from the Sundance Film Festival and the rest derives from sponsors, grants, and private contributions.

Between six and eight fellows for the Feature Film Lab are chosen from more than 3,000 applications and scripts and receive room, board, and equipment at a cost to the organization of up to $75,000 each. In labs that last anywhere from four days to four weeks they get the chance to rehearse, shoot, edit, and rework scenes under the guidance of creative advisers—often institute alumni—and with the input of other fellows, staff, and Redford himself. The goal is to leave the institute with a rough edited reel of four or five scenes from their screenplays, but they take away more. "The experience at the Sundance Institute was a creative epiphany about how to solve my first film," says writer/director Miguel Arteta, whose debut, *Star Maps,* won him a lucrative deal with Fox Searchlight. Arteta's next projects, *Chuck and Buck* and *The Good Girl,* premiered at the Sundance Film Festival and sold to studios.

The institute chooses fellows carefully, as does any organization that relies on its people for energy and ideas. What it is chiefly looking for, Redford says, is "voice." Visionary business leaders—Jobs, Chouinard, Jeff Bezos, Ralph Lauren—bestow something of their characters upon their companies, but as organizations grow their founders' voices grow fainter. In the end, organizations draw their voices (their real voices—not those manufactured by professional brand builders) from their members. In a world of easy imitation, Redford recognizes, voice can be a potent differentiator.

One way the institute staff fosters voice is by selecting fellows based on their raw ideas—scripts, a rough 10 minutes of film— rather than on their resumés. Michelle Satter, director of the feature film program and a guiding force at the Sundance Institute, describes the ideal: "a script or a short film so unique or with a story that hasn't been told, that only that artist could tell."

One thing Satter, who is the architect of the institute process, doesn't weigh is the commercial prospects of an applicant's idea. Indeed, market-focus groups are verboten at Sundance, as perhaps they should be in any business that truly values innovation. Consumer research, says Michael Lehmann, a veteran film director and longtime creative adviser to Sundance, is what makes Hollywood movies Hollywood movies. "Studios are first and foremost market-driven: They work backwards," says Lehmann. "They try to figure out what audiences want and give it to them. Beyond that they're not sure what to do." Sundance reverses the process and begins with the unique visions of the artists it supports.

Then, as they work, fellows are constantly urged away from proven solutions and toward experiments. Granted, it isn't difficult for the institute to encourage risk-taking since it expects no direct financial return from its investment in talent. Still, the Sundance brand is built on developing and promoting work Hollywood wouldn't gamble on: Sundance without risk would cease to be Sundance. So while breakthrough ideas are more common here than at most organizations, so are disappointments and dead ends. And that's okay. "The worst day of this lab, the day you feel you've fallen on your face, will be the best day of the lab because that will be your greatest learning moment," Satter says. "You may fail, you may fly, but you'll move on and learn."

Fellows appreciate that support, and they are also motivated by the many opportunities to have their work seen, which after all is what most creative people want. Sundance has developed multiple platforms, such as the festival, cable channels, and new film series, to showcase innovation wherever it springs up and cheerfully helps fellows make connections outside the Sundance mantle as well. "It's about getting the ideas out, it's about getting the work seen," says Ken Brecher, executive director of the Sundance Institute. "If the work finds its way to a Sundance platform, that's great. If it finds its way to another platform, that's also great."

"The labs and film festival are the twin engines that drive the whole deal," says North Carolina's Pollock. But "the entire Sundance family of organizations is synergistic and holistic. Each entity uniquely builds the value of the whole."

You can learn a lot about an organization by the language people use to describe what they do: whether they speak in acronyms or jargon or generics. The language of Sundance, not surprisingly, reflects its artistic purpose, but also the tools it uses to promote original thinking and inventive solutions to problems. The Sundance lexicon includes sketchpad, generosity, story, conversation, and contradiction—words that are foreign to business but, I believe, fundamental to innovation. Here is how they are used at Sundance.

**Sketchpad:** The Sundance Institute is rugged. Veteran directors haul equipment; movie stars carry their own food and sleep in cabins; everyone moves tables and chairs. The environment is enriched by what is not there as much as by what is. "When I started the institute there was no place for the artists to work," says Redford. "I mean it was raw here. They worked in the ski patrol house, the firehouse, and the maintenance shed. I was kind of embarrassed by what was here, but it was all I could afford to do.

"Later on though," says Redford, "I realized we'd done something very right." The primitive conditions forced the artists to be resourceful, to improvise, to stretch and experiment more fully.

Certainly Sundance could have built the slickest sound stages and editing facilities, but Redford and his staff believe that would push the filmmakers too close too soon to a finished product, and that that threatens originality. "We need to get away from preciousness, of having to have everything right," says Satter. "The workshop scenes [shot by the fellows] are deliberately primitive in terms of production values and design. It is process, not product, that is the cornerstone of the work."

**Contradiction:** A fellow lies on his back on an old couch inside an editing trailer. Hands over face. Exhausted and exhilarated. "You take your medicine and you build on it," he says. Within the last hour, Redford, Arteta, and Lehmann have dropped by, one after the other, to talk about the scene he is trying to cut. Their ideas are great. They also completely contradict one another. As the fellow plays their words over in his head, he gets an inkling of still another approach. His tries it, and that edit is his best yet.

> **We need to get away from preciousness, of having to have everything right.**

At Sundance, contradiction is achieved by exposing fellows to as many perspectives as possible. Each session is attended by between 35 and 40 creative advisers, people like Denzel Washington, Sally Field, Glenn Close, Stanley Tucci, Alexander Payne, Kathryn Bigelow, and Jon Avnet. But rather than working with a single mentor whose approach and opinions they might uncritically absorb, the fellows get the divergent views of a slew of experts and must reconcile them into a vision of their own. They can also move among the institute's various labs—including those for filmmakers, screenwriters, theater directors, and composers—to see how ideas play out in different disciplines.

"We need contradiction to get to truth," says Redford. "Some of the most interesting things we see and feel have contradictory parts. It's a part of our lives. Let's use it rather than push it out and pretend it doesn't exist."

**Generosity:** It's 7:45 p.m. and the sun setting behind the mountains casts a soft blue halo across the canyon. Everyone from the labs—about 75 people—is savoring a hearty communal meal around big round tables in a big white tent. They are talking, laughing, and enjoying one another's company.

Redford would like to be among them. But earlier he'd watched one of the fellows struggling to prepare for a difficult shoot the next day. He'd seen her wrestle with the actors, wrestle with the material; and he'd sensed her confidence was shaken. Reaching for the key to the nearest van, he calls to her across the parking lot: "Let's go scout some different locations for the bus stop shoot tomorrow. There are three sites I want to show you. We can talk about the setups on the way."

Company leaders—particularly the founder and keeper of the vision—can set the tone for how employees behave toward one another. The tone Redford has set is one of generosity. And it is a kind of generosity that sets the table for collaboration.

The long-term yield on generosity is visible. Fellows leave Sundance with a kind of lifetime resource commitment from the institute. Staff often help alumni move their projects into production by running interference with commercial markets, working contacts, and making phone calls to connect artists with casting agents, producers, and sources of financing. Alumni, in turn, come back to Sundance to serve as creative advisers and help tyro innovators with their work. "If you create an atmosphere of freedom, where people aren't afraid someone will steal their ideas, they engage with each other, they help one another," Redford says. "The freedom of not being threatened by your colleagues creates a whole energy."

**Story:** Most evenings around 10 p.m., the institute's staff, fellows, and advisers stroll down to the Owl Bar, a rosewood haven imported from Thermopolis, Wyo., where the real Hole in the Wall Gang hung out more than a century ago. There, they kick back, quaff ice-cold Wasatch ale, and swap stories from earlier sessions: about experiments that succeeded and failed; ingenious solutions to difficult problems; breakthroughs, breakouts, and the occasional breakdown. The purpose of these gatherings is to perpetuate institutional memory and knowledge. A task that most organizations either undervalue or ignore, Sundance achieves—characteristically—by returning to the oral tradition.

Redford says that storytelling is as important for today's businesses as it was for the Ute tribes that once inhabited this land. Organizations with no knowledge of their own stories borrow cheesy imitations from the media or steal them from competitors (that is why so much advertising appears interchangeable). And Redford believes storytelling can be fostered by the design and flow of an organization's social and community habits, like the informal gatherings at the Owl Bar. "I think any culture without mythology and storytelling is doomed," says Redford. "Stories are a way of communicating, a way of keeping certain things alive."

**Conversation:** In preparation for my visit to Sundance I listened to 100 hours of taped interviews with Redford. When I arrived we walked together around the village, and I watched him collaborate with staff members and artists throughout the week. And here's the remarkable thing: In all that time, I never heard him repeat himself. Even when I would read back to him his own words for clarification (a process that usually makes people self-aware) Redford was uninterested—he was already on to the next idea.

> "If you create an atmosphere of freedom, where people aren't afraid someone will steal their ideas, they engage with each other, they help one another."

While most people, especially people in business situations, use conversation as a forum for presenting themselves, Redford uses conversation to become himself: He intends to be different when it is over. Just talking with him is a lesson in shaking off old ways of thinking. Like a chess player, he sees the whole picture, follows the moves, and finds the connections before you know where you're going—then he turns the board. If you're lost, he turns it to give you a leg up. If you're safe, he turns it to keep you fresh.

Management theorists stress the importance of conducting companywide conversations but not of having leaders who are great conversationalists. At Sundance no one asks a question to which he or she already knows the answer. Words and ideas move in one direction only—forward.

It's not as though business doesn't recognize the importance of organic growth—corporate annual reports routinely proclaim a commitment to innovation. But it's not showing up anywhere else. "The innovation right now in business—as far as I can tell—is coming out of paper and air," says Redford. "The signs are everywhere. The collapsing of certain corporate structures, the mergers, the consolidation that was supposed to beef up profit are clearly, by and large, not working."

**"I don't believe in endgames... except the one that's forced on you."**

Innovation at most companies is pursued with desperate, random acts or unevolved strategies; or it is so incremental and predictable that it isn't really innovation at all. Sundance, by contrast, doesn't just encourage innovation—it ensures that it happens by process and design. Most companies won't find it a stretch to imitate at least some of Redford's tactics. Expose people to a variety of conflicting perspectives. Hire for raw ideas. Throw innovators back on their own resources. Perpetuate institutional memory. Allow for experimentation, mistakes, and dead ends. Employ short-term mentors. Don't respond slavishly to market research. Engage in conversations that lead to new conclusions rather than persuade people of foregone ones. Periodically switch environments. And if you are the company leader, give generously to innovators of your time and attention.

Perhaps most important, make clear that you yourself are on a quest for the genuinely new and that—like Redford—if you achieve that quest you will immediately start searching all over again. "There's no endgame at Sundance; there's not meant to be," says Redford. "It's still evolving and it's meant to keep evolving.

"I don't believe in endgames," says Redford, "except the one that's forced on you."

# 12
## *The Mad Dogs,*
## *Dreamers and Sages*

# Giving Blessing

**Maya Angelou**
*Poet, teacher, leader*

*We are more alike, my friends, than we are unalike.*

Maya Angelou uses language as a consummate grown up to give direction, assurance, exhortation . . . and blessing. If you've heard Dr. Angelou speak, you know what I mean. She is an artist in many fields—poet, film-maker, dancer, director, and performer, but her greatest art is that of giving "benediction," good strong words that send people forth to make a difference in their world. She has a genius for doing this both in individual conversations and to swelling crowds in great auditoriums. It is a gift that clearly grows with age and use.

Angelou's home and web of connection has become a palpable exchange of energy and influence for myriad civic groups: women's health, arts, African-American history, human rights, education, and literacy. The pace of her schedule for writing, performing, interviewing, and hosting is remarkable.

The day I met with Dr. Angelou, she had awakened to write at 4:30, had already sat for a photo session for *National Geographic,* and met with a representative from UNICEF; and it was only nine o'clock in the morning! Yet when she turned toward me as we spoke, she brought a quality of personal energy that was extraordinary. She addressed me by my full name, asked me as many questions as I asked her, and conveyed to me a deeper sense of the importance of my own work than I could have imagined.

When I asked about her personal resources, where she finds the energy and power she brings to the countless causes and relationships in which she is invested, she stopped and shook her head with slow surprise as if to explain that if she had to tell me, I'd never understand it. "To whom much is given, much is required," she said. "That is what our lives must be about, giving back."

Angelou's role as a word-giver for contemporary culture is especially striking in light of her own period of muteness as a child. As an eight year-old girl, she was raped and so physically injured that she was taken to the emergency room. She refused to name her attacker, fearing for the man's life if he was found out. The night after her brother Bailey finally pulled the truth from her, the man was found kicked to death in a bar; and Maya Johnson vowed never to speak again.

Overcome by the power of her own words, Angelou held her silence until adolescence, when an English teacher encouraged her to memorize the words of great poets and to speak through them. Today, Angelou is a great conversationalist and a brilliant raconteur, and her words are never small. She speaks with the power of a poet and addresses the needs of brokenness.

When Angelou tells her story, however, it is never a story of scarcity. Hers is the story of a young girl, who, despite growing up in hard times, knew she was cared for by generous and wise elders. Angelou's books and poems chronicle an ongoing exchange of vision, responsibility, and ideas among the people who have blessed her. From her brother Bailey, Angelou got a sense that she could do anything; from her grandmother she got a certainty that she must do it well; and from her mother she got the possibility of doing it all with elegance.

She passes these blessings on to all who enter her circle, whether friend, beneficiary, or grateful reader. In doing so, she takes part in  a rich cycle of ongoing growth, beginning with generosity and leading to gratitude.

# *Real Imagination*

### Ralph Ardill
*Marketing and Strategic Planning Director,*
*Imagination*

*We have more products and less difference,*
*more information and less time. Each idea must*
*communicate to our senses on a multitude of*
*levels.*

Ralph Ardill's company, Imagination, is one of the world's most highly regarded design consultancies. It is a pioneer in the area of brand experiences, a new and powerful approach for connecting brands with consumers and corporations. Says Ardill,

We think about experiential design in terms of not only physicality for the place, but the design of the story around that place, how it comes into being and becomes adopted by people. You're designing a methodology, which often is the message.

I think that there is a big backlash. For a long time there's been a lot of thinking about brands, trying to bring consumers into the world of the brand. So you would go to a theme park and everything would be themed and you would be in this kind of imaginary brand world, which would take you out of your real life and put you somewhere else. There is a fundamental shift coming where brands now have to look at how they can find a place in the lives of people, rather than trying to create places where people can live in their world.

Imagination's headquarters in London are an experience in their own right. The Imagination building was transformed from the ruins of an Edwardian school into one of the most exciting buildings in London. The feel is like being backstage during the development of a theatrical performance. Architects, lighting and sound designers, model makers, photographers, filmmakers, graphic artists of all kind mix it up, argue, debate, create energy and great ideas on a daily basis. According to Ardill,

There is a big mind shift, particularly for older companies who have almost become empires. They have ruled and dominated and created—and gone out unconquered. As we know, empires fall. So how does the phoenix rise again? It will rise up in a different form. It will have a certain set of behavioral traits that people will recognize, but it will come to you in a different way. I think that's good. I personally get a lot more engaged by things that I feel I don't have to applaud—that I feel it's okay to question.

I think brands often miss that point completely. They want to create flawless perfect pieces of communication. Again, it's about being human. People argue. People disagree. People are idiosyncratic. People have bad days. People don't always tell the truth—sometimes because they don't want to hurt someone's feelings, sometimes because they do.

This kind of humanization of brands and organizations really needs to be connected to corporate behavior and brand communications.

As Aldous Huxley said, "Experience is not what happens to you, it is what you make of what happens to you."

# Working from Scratch

## Nancy Beach
*Director of Programming*
*Willow Creek Community Church*

*We are limited human beings who often wrestle with voices that say there are no more ideas, our blank sheet of paper will stay blank, and we can't create.*

When Nancy Beach was a teenager, she belonged to a youth group that rented a movie theater in South Barrington, Illinois, to begin a new kind of church. Bill Hybels, the group leader, preached; and Nancy and other members put together the programs, no choirs or hymnals, but contemporary band music, drama, and art. That youth group, which grew into Willow Creek Community Church, is now the largest church in North America. It has revolutionized the way church is conceived around the world.

As the long-time director of programming at Willow Creek, Nancy's rethinking of church programming is recalibrating every assumption we have about worship. After twenty years, the Willow Creek team still begins each planning session for a weekend service with a blank page. Beach is accustomed to working from scratch.

There are no givens for the worship hour. Willow Creek hosts the same weekend service on Saturday nights and three times on Sunday morning, but the services one week will look nothing like the week before. They use every imaginable aspect of the arts, short seven minute dramas, contemporary solos, multi-media, dance, and combinations in between.

Though Hybels' sermons are still usually the center of the worship hour, Beach's team designs the service around the goal of seeding transformational moments into the service. Their aim is to re-create the surprise and wonder of being lost and being found in a relevant service organized around thoughtful, artistic moves.

Designing these moments—and keeping them fresh— demands an ongoing process of following the ideas of each team member out far enough to see if the idea will catch fire, as well as passing the torch of creativity easily and effectively throughout the parts of the team. Beach and her team are ever-turning artists, always on the lookout for new sources of creative ideas—from Broadway to Disneyworld.

But Willow Creek faces a challenge much greater than any theatre or theme park. Besides bringing creativity and excellence to their productions, Beach's team has to bring authenticity—and they must bring it fresh each week. Beach believes that the make-or-break criteria for each service is, *Is it real?*

> When I observe music, teaching, video, drama, or any other part of the hour on Sunday, do I believe it down to my toes or is something getting in my way of trusting what is being communicated? We do not serve attenders well if we think it's best to ignore reality, to pretend that Christians don't struggle with parenting, marriage, ethics in the workplace, financial challenges, anger, lust, guilt, pride, greed, loneliness, and fear of failure. Rather, we need to identify with the realities of the human condition and with the world we all live in Monday through Saturday.

What Beach has found is that great creativity relies on a million things that can go wrong—art, movement, volunteers, emotion, and people. Like high-wire work, they do it live and they do it without many props. And the next week they start all over again.

# An Elegant Cordee

**Denise Scott Brown and Robert Venturi**
*Architects*
*Venturi Scott Brown & Associates*

*You don't try to be visionary. The more you try for it, the less likely it is you'll attain it. Being truly visionary is being profoundly of now. If you deal with the now perceptively, you deal with the future automatically.*

Great climbers are always talking about the virtues of the cordee, the pairing of soul mates bound together by a rope. It is the perfect partnership that destiny intertwines to scale the great summits, the union that allows each to climb much better than they could apart, enhancing each other's strengths and complimenting each other's weaknesses.[1]

Venturi's artistic brilliance linked with Scott Brown's visionary courage has led us to vistas unreachable without their stunning discoveries. In their presence you feel the excitement of being on a great adventure as they move around the difficult terrain of complex and contradictory ideas and problems with grace. Such are their supreme skills.

Denise Scott Brown's elegant manner and distinctive voice would make her a better Isak Denison than Meryl Streep, while Venturi's confident presence would make him an imposing John Chancellor understudy. Together this genteel pair stands at the summit of contemporary American architecture, having earned an international reputation as a leading architectural design and planning team. Through work in these disciplines as well as the decorative arts and theoretical writing, they have been shaping forces in contemporary design.

When Venturi received the Pritzker Prize, architecture's highest honor, Paul Goldberger of the *New Yorker* wrote "No architect is more deserving of this honor…he put forth a set of ideas that provided an intellectual basis for a thousand different themes by a thousand different architects."[2]

Herbert Muschamp, architecture critic for the *New York Times* said, "If the Prizker were as distinguished an award as it's cracked up to be, it would be a scandal that Venturi had to wait in line behind such lesser talents as Philip Johnson and I.M. Pie and that the prize was not made jointly to Scott Brown, his partner of 25 years."[3]

Their portfolio of buildings includes The Sainsbury Wing of the National Gallery in London and contemporary art museums in Seattle and San Diego, as well as buildings on the campuses of Harvard, Princeton, Dartmouth, Penn, Yale, and the Universities of Michigan and California.

We spent the morning exploring Venturi and Scott Brown's latest completed work, the new Frist Campus Center on the campus of Princeton University. Palmer Hall, the former austere physics lab had been transformed to create a vibrant communal campus center. The result juxtaposes its original Jacobean style with modern communication and iconography. Soaring atrium spaces, stylized graffiti, neon signage, LED screens, and projection video serve as important vehicles for communication and community.

The building really works. They have finally solved the problem of finding out about the great lecture you just missed by providing the information electronically before, not after, an event.

Then we set out in a driving rainstorm to meet Venturi and Scott Brown at their Philadelphia headquarters to look into the nature of their extraordinary imaginative intelligence.

# Creative Warrior

## Fu-Ding Cheng
### *Filmmaker, Artist, Shaman*

*Is your focus on painting the leaves green or watering the roots?*

Fu-Ding Cheng is an artist and shamanic filmmaker who has spent the last twenty-five years on a personal quest involving Buddhist meditation, treks in the Himalayas, Chinese Kung Fu, and Toltec wisdom traditions, among others. The focus of his work is personal freedom and self-illumination. Based in Venice, California, his innovative art house video films have been seen at the Whitney Museum in New York City and at many international film festivals.

Cheng's abiding interest in consciousness and its ability to take us to fantastic places, if we let it, are exemplified in his film stories such as *Zen Tails for the Urban Explorer* and *The Winged Cage.* In the latter, Cheng considers the spirit of a man who is trapped in a moving cage. He trundles awkwardly around the city by day, but his soul escapes at night, thanks to the loosening of his inhibitions and the awakening of a zesty, lyrical imagination.

When we first met, Fu-Ding was a visiting professor at the North Carolina School of the Arts. During his time here, Cheng shared a story with me:

There's a valley full of hard working people. They spend all their time tending to the trees, working tirelessly and earnestly against a never-ending cycle. Their jobs are to paint the leaves of the trees green. The leaves keep turning brown so fast that they can barely keep up. A sage comes to the valley and observes this folly. He seeks out the leaders and speaks of looking beyond the surface to where the real action is, of tending the roots, treating the soil, of nutrients and interconnections in the environment. The leaders and the workers are so exhausted from the stress, they ignore him, they have no time, and they are barely keeping the leaves painted green as it is.

That's the way it is with imagination, people don't take it seriously. Our minds are a factory of dreams. But our impulses, instincts, and ability to dream have become ossified. A patina has formed on our ability to see things beyond one way. The mind's natural state is creative. We need to cleanse our components, and start working on the roots. Get beyond the narrow band and connect to the broadband, the huge spectrum of possibilities.

Imagination is our ultimate power tool!

# Taking a Full Swing

**Joan Darling**
*Writer, director, actress, producer*

*To get artists to take a full swing, you need to educate them, love them and seduce them into it. They need to allow themselves to go all the way to the end of their skulls in their own imagination.*

Joan Darling's capacity for daring associations, along with her sense of humor and her insight into the human predicament has had a palpable effect on the shape of the American entertainment industry.

With a shrewd eye and uncanny ear, Emmy-recipient Darling has given us some of the funniest moments in TV history, directing ground-breaking episodes of shows like *MASH, Taxi, Rhoda, The Mary Tyler Moore Show,* and *The Dick van Dyke Show.*

My personal favorite was her one-of-a kind soap opera, *Mary Hartmann, Mary Hartmann.* For me that show marks the day TV began seeing the world differently, not as we thought it should be, but as it really looks from whatever odd angle you are considering it in a given moment. With that shift, TV got funnier, and so did the world. I'll never forget stopping by my grandparents' house one summer afternoon and hearing my grandmother's muffled gasps coming from the pantry. My grandmother was in there watching *Mary Hartmann, Mary Hartmann* where my grandfather couldn't see her and trying to contain her laughter.

During my time at the Sundance Institute, I had a chance to see Joan Darling at work as a creative advisor, exercising her genius at encouraging the creative process. More recently, I visited her new home in Chapel Hill where she and her husband have just signed on for a three-year teaching stint. It was no surprise to hear that she swept the field in student evaluations her first semester.

Ask any student or colleague of Darling's, past or present, those who worked with her for a week at Sundance or a semester or an episode to tell you about her, and they'll smile big and start telling tales. She's irrepressibly fun, giving everyone a chance to take their best swing. But she confided to me, that it's the ones with guts and an unusual perspective that keep her going. "It's only the oddballs that we get the good stuff from."

> **It's only the oddballs that we get the good stuff from.**

# Embracing Contraries

**Peter Elbow**
*Professor of English*
*University of Massachusetts-Amherst*

*I believe that everyone can write with power*
*and eloquence given an occasion of urgency and*
*permission to do so.*

Peter Elbow is an English professor. He's tall and somewhat gangly; he loves to wear all shades of green—and mixes his greens in indiscriminate ways. Sometimes it hurts your eyes.

At the thought of an English teacher, whether his greens match or not, many of us are transported back to junior high and the days of getting back compare and contrast essays covered with red ink comments such as *Awk, Redundant,* or *Sloppy Thinking.* We have flashbacks of grammar abuse. Elbow knows about that.

He's a recovering English victim himself. Like most kids, he started out liking words, playing with the way they sound and they fit together. Inspired by an English teacher in high school, Elbow studied English literature at Oxford and finally went on to Harvard for a Ph.D. in Chaucer. But somewhere in the middle of this process, he stopped writing.

Surrounded by English teachers asking for papers, complete sentences, well-defended theses, and bibliographies, he "lost his starch" as they say in the South. He crumbled. He started papers, then threw them away, and pretty soon couldn't even start them. When he couldn't even write good excuses for not writing, he dropped out. He had failed.

What he didn't do, however, was lie about it. He kept teaching English, but he faced the fact that he was an English teacher who couldn't write. His book *Writing Without Teachers* is the story of his own process of figuring out how to write when he was scared to death. It turns out that just about everyone, except for Bill Buckley and Danielle Steele, is scared to death of writing. It was a best-seller.

What Elbow discovered is that if you start out planning to write something perfect, you'll never get off first base. In its early stages, writing must take risks. It's the bad writing that gets to the good writing.

Elbow has found traditional teaching environments are often inhospitable to the kind of confidence we need to write. In academics we all get schooled in the doubting game. Scientific method is the triumph of doubting, but we forget how to believe. Doubt is important, we need a crap-detector, but it's also limiting. Doubt can easily trump our capacity to believe, to try, to hope.

Elbow talks about two kinds of thinking: first order and second order thinking. *First order thinking* is creative and intuitive, looking for big ideas or interesting paths, but not yet trying to pin anything down. We use it when we're getting started on an idea or trying to follow a hunch. Elbow calls this eating like an owl. An owl swallows a mouse whole, then after a few minutes, it coughs up a little ball of fur and bones that it can't use.

**An owl swallows a mouse whole, then after a few minutes, it coughs up a little ball of fur and bones that it can't use.**

*Second order thinking* is much more controlled and sequenced. We're steering for certainty, efficiency, and exactness. Ironically, in our urgency about being efficient and exact, we often forfeit the power and intuition that comes from a good first swing.

Elbow believes in a process he calls free writing, writing fast and hard for a short period of time with no plan, no grades, not even an audience. It's a way of getting the stuff to the paper before we try to control it. It gives us a space in which we can say the wrong thing to get to the right thing; a space in which we try out risky stuff because we know we'll be allowed to recover our own fumbles. As he puts it, "Being 'promiscuous' and sleeping with the wildest range of ideas (in the safety of provisionality) gives us the best chance of finding out what's actually in our mind and deciding what to keep and what to throw out."[1]

In the invention stage of the writing process, the writer needs to believe that the little corner of an idea he is holding on to or the little ray of light that has flickered across his thinking might eventually lead him to something more. He needs to drop the heavy cargo of doubt and follow his ideas without worrying about where they're taking him or how the writing will look when it's finished.

Elbow tells writers to ignore the old English teacher that sits on their shoulder telling them that they are wasting their time or using poor grammar. A writer needs to listen hard to the murmur of promise as he follows his ideas. Many of us have had teachers who were known for sniffing out error in our work; a few of us have had teachers who were good at sniffing out possibility. Elbow asks us to write for the good-sniffing teacher.

# A Different Voice

**Carol Gilligan**
*Professor of Psychology*
*Harvard University*

> *When I hear my work being cast in terms of*
> *whether women or men are really (essentially)*
> *different or who is better than whom, I know that I*
> *have lost my voice, because these are not my questions.*
> *Instead, my questions are about our perceptions of*
> *reality and truth: how we know, how we hear, how*
> *we see, how we speak.*

While a graduate student at Harvard in the early seventies, psychologist Carol Gilligan worked as a research assistant to renowned psychologist Lawrence Kohlberg, who had developed a new theory of moral development. One of the new women on the block, Gilligan began to notice the ways that the academic research systems of her field were failing to allow for differences between men and women.

What Gilligan began to discover in her research was that for many women the traditional questions Kohlberg had devised didn't fit their answers. For instance, Kohlberg had constructed a scenario for studying human morality that involved the dilemma of a man named Heinz who had to decide whether to steal a drug he could not afford in order to save the life of his wife. The study was oriented around the idea that one's morality becomes more universalized as one develops.

Gilligan noticed that the girls in her study seemed to understand the study's assumptions, while at the same time resisting them. The boys she studied tended to think about the dilemma abstractly, whereas the girls tended to think about it relationally. And they resisted making universal decisions about it. They seemed to base their answers on the relationship between factors, not a prioritizing of their importance. In short, they said, "*It depends!*" This was a breakthrough observation in 1982, when Gilligan published her book, *In a Different Voice: Psychological Theory and Women's Development*.

When I talked to Gilligan in the summer of 2003, twenty-one years after the book came out, it was against a backdrop of ongoing and escalating furor. In many ways, the challenges to Gilligan's intentions and methodology are immaterial now. Her early attention to the differences between men and women and the ways that psychology had tried to understand them has irreversibly changed the conversation of her discipline. And she was not alone. At the time Gilligan was writing, people were simultaneously turning on the lights in academic disciplines across the board. From history to biology to art, the reality was breaking through: *In our most brilliant centers of scholarships, university departments devoted to exploring human experience, the men had been leaving out the women, and so had the women!*

Carol Gilligan has spent her life "talking back" to the arrangements of academic thinking that left women out of the picture. Not surprisingly, both her work and her person have been caricaturized by people who have found them challenging. What surprised me when I finally met her was how much of that caricaturization had sifted into my own expectations.

Though I've appreciated Gilligan's work, I realize now that I still expected her to be unnatural. I had pictured a woman who was sober and intense or maybe a little swoony, somewhere between Henry Kissinger and Cher.

My first glimpse of her fit my expectation. Sitting on the steps of the small, round room where she'd be speaking, she looked like a very smart, grown up hippie. She had on a long black skirt and sandals, and at sixty-eight, still looked every bit the dancer she is.

Once the program began, however, she began to wiggle and stretch like a kid at a piano recital; but with this big exception, Gilligan seemed to be stretching towards the discussion and wiggling, not from boredom, but from pleasure. Pleasure that this group of people had come to hear her, pleasure in her own muscled and supple body, pleasure in the things she was preparing to tell us.

Her shoes were off, and she was rubbing the tops of her tanned, bare feet along the metal rungs of the chair in front of her as if she was testing her bath water. When she was finally introduced, she smiled grandly like a kid about to blow out her candles and stepped to the center of the room. She was pumped.

At that point, if she'd begun her talk with an arabesque or a somersault or a chorus of *Ninety-Nine Bottles of Beer on the Wall,* I wouldn't have been surprised. There is nothing angry or rigid about her. In fact, Carol Gilligan may be the most visibly joyful grownup I have ever seen.

# Sound Frontiers

## Chris Hardman

*Founder and Artistic Director, Antenna Theater*

*The reason sound design is so powerful is that our ears are our first line of defense. Your ears never go to sleep. They tell you there's danger, someone's behind you. Our ears are our early warning system.*

According to Chris Hardman, the date he and I first met was actually 13,200,002,002. He advocates that we all begin to use this new All Time calendar because he questions the significance of the arbitrarily conceived Gregorian calendar 2003 year mark, or the Hebrew calendar year 5763, or the Chinese year 4701, or the Islamic year 1423 when, in fact the universe is 15 billion years old. Common convenience, habit, and usage are the only reasons we continue to use them. Hardman believes our new knowledge of the beginning of time since the Big Bang leads to an exciting proposition.

Consider the magnitude of the shift if we change the way people commonly think about their place in the universe in the continuum of time. "Think of it this way. If you were to walk 13,000 feet along a beach, (we do just that in his experience called Sands of Time) the last three grains of sand would represent five thousand years. In other words, all of recorded human history would be reduced to a tiny drop in a very large bucket."

Chris Hardman is the founder and artistic director of the San Francisco-based Antenna Theater. A pioneer in the use of Walkman technology in theater, Hardman used the techniques developed by his theater company to launch Antenna Audio, now the world's largest audio tour company. Antenna is designated as a theater only because they create public events that are held at certain times at specific locations. But these may be the only elements a particular event has in common with other theaters.

Receive. Transform. Transmit. That's Hardman's unique method. His mission is to invent, discover, and explore new ways of involving a variety of artistic disciplines and new technologies in experiential productions. The *audient*, his term for the individual participating audience member, is an active and integral part of the creative production. Antenna has pioneered new

**Receive. Transform. Transmit.**

experiential formats involving Walkmans, infrared-transmitted sound, sensor-tripped animation, interactive video, and multi-channel radio transmission. He fuses storytelling with ever-evolving technology, with live performance, public art, and interaction with the community in which his experiments are created and presented.

In the transmission you may become Andy Warhol, a homeless person waiting in line for soup, a student waiting to enter the principal's office, the lone bombardier at the seminal moment flying over Hiroshima; or, as I was introduced to the experience, Samuel Taylor Coleridge writing a poem in an opium-induced dream state.

All my encounters with Hardman have felt like episodes of *The X–Files*, strange characters, unusual places, a syncopated rhythm of encounters. It's like music in a pentatonic scale; you can only play the black keys.

Today's encounter starts like all the others. I cross the Golden Gate Bridge from San Francisco and exit towards Sausalito, but wait . . . instead of heading into town, I am instructed to double back . . . proceed slowly . . . onto Bunker road . . . through a narrow one-way tunnel . . . I wait at a five-minute red light for clearance. Enter the Marin Headlands. Past abandoned military installations, shrouded in thick fog, the brilliant sun on the other side of the bay slips away . . . day turns into night, and it's only early afternoon!   Now on a gravel road, a row of dozens of identical army huts. There are no people. The valley seems abandoned in time.   Find the ocean shop . . . a nondescript building number 1057 marks the spot. Obey all signs within the environs. Thank you for not smoking.

# Knowledge Entrepreneur

### T George Harris
*Journalist and Past Editor-in-Chief of Psychology Today*

*From medicine to the Internet, the capacity
to originate an idea, a tune, a cure for a disease,
a web site, whatever, has become the most valued
talent in most human endeavors.*

T George Harris has used his reporter's eye and network of contemporary thinkers to develop a series of high-level platforms for addressing the issues of our times.

As a reporter in the sixties he developed his ability to read the times and the people who drove them. In a time when few people cultivated friendships across the color line, Harris met weekly with Alaine Locke, the first African-American Rhodes Scholar, for tutoring on what Harris calls "Black Light." Harris was drawn to the centers of racial conflict during these times because he believed that people could sort things out if they knew the facts and could understand each other.

In 1952, the year before its historic Brown vs. the Board of Education decision, the Supreme Court handed down five questions addressing the practical questions of how American schools might be integrated. Through Alaine Locke, Harris had come to know the "Black Cabinet" of Washington, which was comprised of the single black advisor buried in each major governmental department since FDR's administration. When Harris got hold of the Court's questions, he called Dr. James

Calliver, research chief of the then tiny Office of Education to ask him if they had the research necessary to keep the decision from stalling out for lack of data.

Calliver said, "George, nowhere in the government does anyone have the capacity or the will to answer those questions." There was a long silence, after which Harris said, "Dr. Calliver, how many of the Black Cabinet can you bring to my apartment tonight?" Calliver brought four men to Harris's little bachelor apartment, and they laid plans, and hammered out letters for funding on Harris's old Royal portable.

The newborn Fund for the Republic put up the money, and Harris suggested that his friend Harry Ashmore, editor of the *Arkansas Gazette* be asked to head the study. In record time, by a means Harris says he never wanted to know, each useful piece of research was slipped to the Justices. In advance of the decision, the full two-volume Ashmore Report was delivered to every Southern editor.

When the Brown decision was announced, and was to be implemented with "all deliberate speed," the fastest level of action possible, much of our nation was stunned and all of our school systems were unprepared. The Ashmore report, however, served as a great resource for the process, not only reducing bloodshed, but also giving a heads-up to those who would listen and a head-start to those who would be making the decision work.

In the sixties, Harris was everywhere. He was with James Meredith when he first talked through the Ole Miss riot, and he was often the only white reporter with whom Elijah Muhammad would meet.

T George Harris managed the flux and flow of working at the center of the sixties', seventies', and eighties' "Age of Psychology" with the same discerning eye and the belief that people want to understand one another. What he offered to his writers and his readers was a meaningful frame and a sense of contextuality, while at the same time helping them develop their own crisp, independent pictures of their field.

When a writer came to La Jolla to work on an issue about women for his *Careers Today* magazine, he was quick to see that her topic was bigger than his magazine; and the concept for *Ms. Magazine* was tested by women in the beach community nearby. Their work on the article led to *Ms. Magazine*.

He was walking down a street in Manhattan listening to Dan Goleman talk about his graduate project on emotional intelligence, when he stopped and said, "Dan, this is not an academic paper you're talking about. This is a *Psychology Today* article, and it may be book. You need to start it now." If Harris backed Gloria Steinem with feminist research and Dan Goleman with his sense of urgency, what did he lend Margaret Mead? His guesthouse, where Mead basked in the admiration of *Psychology Today* writers and artists—and Harris's great sense of fun.

Sam Keen, Gail Sheehy, Marshall McLuhan, Peter Drucker, Warren Bennis, and James Hillman—the list of Harris's writing and thinking partners is legendary. What he offered these individuals was a medium, a lens, a conversation, and a relationship in which they could develop their ideas. And, in each case, their ideas turned out to be so big that they could not have been born without a big frame to welcome them.

Harris has called into being a "roundtable" of hundreds of knowledge entrepreneurs. His perfect pitch for sounding out what's about to emerge culturally, as well as the ability to sense the distinction between tectonic changes and pop culture trends, keeps the conversation at a high level of relevancy.

The multiple and ongoing publications, fields of inquiry, and conversations that continue around Harris's start-ups give testimony to the real possibilities for diverse growth when it is managed by an individual with a sharply-tuned imagination. Harris could see the thing behind the thing, the author behind the person, the book behind the idea, and the audience behind it all.

# Brand Soul

## Joe McCarthy
*Chief Executive Officer*
*McCarthy Mambro Bertino*

*I believe real brands have a soul. I would argue that there are only a few dozen or so real brands with a soul. There are a lot more commodities than there are true brands. Brands with soul appeal holistically to higher level needs and desires. They transcend and are not bound by the rules, conventions, and limitations of their categories.*

*I don't mean to sound too spiritual but that's a piece of it. It's the difference between Marvin Gaye and Michael Bolton. One is real and singing from his soul and the other is a commercial version of Marvin Gaye.*

Growth and innovation are driven by big ideas. Big ideas create change. Change is the status quo. Change requires risk. Risk requires movement. Movement requires energy. Energy fuels intrinsic passion. Passion creates ideas. That's the new physics of innovation according to Joe McCarthy

Joe McCarthy is the CEO of a new advertising agency headquartered in Boston. He is the former Global Advertising Director at Nike, one of the world's most vital and dynamic brands. During his tenure at Nike, the brand more than doubled in size. On his watch Nike created some of the most highly acclaimed advertising and communications ever seen. The kind of brilliant work that permeates through and actually becomes part of the fabric of the pop culture itself.

McCarthy's start-up agency opened two years ago in the teeth of the most gripping retrenchments the communications and media businesses have ever experienced, and is one of the hottest shops in the country.

I drove through the gray haze of concrete dust and the maze of orange cones at the mouth of the "Big Dig" in the south end of Boston, to a converted piano-manufacturing warehouse, where I spent a week with Joe McCarthy and his high-octane team. The agency experience is an energizing mix—part think tank and part creative brawl.

"Too often companies try to rationally argue the loyalty out of customers, but what makes them come back when the other guy is cheaper? If these rational features aren't coupled with emotionally based communications then the brand doesn't have a true soul and runs a very real risk of being reduced to a commodity," says McCarthy.

Great communications help keep a brand fresh, relevant, vital, and growing.

# Being Jane Fulton Suri

**Jane Fulton Suri**
*Director of Human Factors Design and Research*
*IDEO*

*We've relied tremendously on people's ability to express things verbally as if checking boxes in a questionnaire really gives us insight. There are so many more forms of expression available to us that people engage with everyday. I mean you can't help it, we're physical beings, we represent ourselves physically all the time. So tuning into that is very enlightening.*

Jane Fulton Suri looks like a scientist, not the rats-in-cages type in gloves and white lab coats, but the Jane Goodall type in jeans and a T-shirt. Knowing the inevitable effect she has on the species she studies, she follows them into their natural environments, watching for clues to the nature of their lives. Fulton Suri's subjects are people. She brings to her research the British gift for observation. (Remember Sherlock Holmes and Dr. Johnson's Boswell?) Tom Kelly, Gereral Manager of IDEO, describes Fulton Suri as IDEO's secret weapon, "part anthropologist and seer, as well as good-old-foreign correspondent."

Hyper-observation and synthesis are critical to Suri's kind of research. She believes the proliferation of bad design that surrounds us today is a result of ineffective research. Fueled by an innate curiosity about why people do the things they do, she looks at what people actually do, not what they *say* they do.

Fulton Suri stresses the importance of catching people in their real actions and of transplanting the truths of her observations into life forms—stories. "Stories are the way we make sense of human beings, the way we make sense of the world. Weaving a story through time is one of the ways we receive the wisdom of our tribe. When we go out into the world, we come back with stories; they hold great weight at IDEO."

Jane Fulton Suri leads the Worldwide Human Factors Design and Research team at IDEO, the legendary international award-winning design and development firm with hundreds of cutting-edge products and services.

> **Stories are the way we make sense of human beings, the way we make sense of the world.**

Fulton Suri pioneered IDEO's human-centered design approach that involves the use of observation in context, empathic and projective methods, experience prototyping, and iterative testing as part of the design process. For Fulton Suri, design is not a noun; it's a verb.

To fully experience Fulton Suri's soft-spoken nuance and subtlety, one must listen carefully to this petite woman. Fulton Suri was one of my first stops when I set out on the *Odyssey Project,* and I revisited her Human Factors lab in Pier 28 under the Bay Bridge in San Francisco a year later to see what new concepts she was on to. IDEO is continually developing and evolving their techniques to better understand people, their experiences, perceptions, and needs, all with the idea of inspiring and guiding their design work in ways that resonate with the people who will encounter it.

Fulton Suri explains some of their new techniques:

**Cognitive maps**: We simply ask people to represent their perception of real or virtual space and show how they navigate through it. This is a useful way to discover the significant pathways, landmarks, and other features that figure into a person's experience.

**Collage-making**: This is another method that involves asking participants to create something from their own experience. It's based on selecting from large collections of images; it helps us make a deeper level of inquiry into more emotional territory. Images tend to evoke personal dreams and memories, providing a forum for expression that may be difficult simply through conversation.

**Bodystorming**: This takes brainstorming to a whole new level by involving physical enactment. We set up a scenario, role playing specific people in a specific place and often with rudimentary props. The physical enactment enables us to draw upon a new level of dynamic inspiration by focus on the intuitive responses participants make.

I'm really interested in this kind of physical learning. It's been fascinating to me to see how archeologists are suddenly understanding more about our ancestors, their tools, and rituals by actually going through enactments in this way.

# *Head Games*

## Richard Tait and Whit Alexander
*Founders*
*The Cranium Company*

*In this time of web alienation the reality is people are fundamentally social animals. They long to get together with friends and family; they want to have a great time; they want to look smart and laugh together; they want to connect with their own talents and have a richer understanding of their friends and families. That's the dynamic we tapped into.*

–Whit Alexander

While the world rushed to go virtual, two ex-Microsoft guys, Richard Tait and Whit Alexander, decided to go real, into the greatest experience ever created: real, physical, connective human relationships.

Born in Scotland, Richard Tait was a *BUM* at Microsoft, a Business Unit Manager heading up the references businesses. He and Whit Alexander first met while working on solving logistical launch issues for the *Encarta World Atlas*. "Microsoft was a fantastic proving ground; it gave us the ability to understand a space and need in the market and how to iteratively work with customers to dial in and create the best possible experience in this space," says Tait.

In an era of increased globalization and homogenized efficiency, people holed up in cubicles, and tethered by E-mail are feeling the backlash of Internet alienation. Could the space that is unfulfilled be the soul . . . real human contact . . .relationship . . . tangible fun missing from people's lives?

Tait and Alexander are the founders of the Cranium Company, the organization that created a best selling board game, *Cranium,* and a series of other games. The two set out to research a void in leisure activity, asking the question,

> Why hasn't there been a huge, runaway hit board game in about 15 years? We saw nothing that seemed to be delivering on the moment, on where we are in society. The huge hit games have been in response to social change. Monopoly was in the Depression, an era where people needed to fantasize about being wealthy. Trivial Pursuit was a push back from the rise of cable television and the decline in network television; people wanted to get together and celebrate in a social setting.

The next challenge came when they finished the game in June and pulled the trigger on their first manufacturing run. "We didn't know that all of the toy buying decisions take place in February, and when we started to go to retailers with the game they told us we'd missed the buying season for Christmas," said Tait.

Sitting together in Starbucks lamenting their most excellent mistake over a double latte, the duo had their second epiphany. Recalls Tate, "We knew who our core customer was. We called them 'dating yuppsters,' people in their mid twenties to late thirties, looking for social connection. There they were—in line at Starbucks. So why don't we take the game to where our customers are rather than where games are sold?"

They started to strategize on an alternative distribution strategy that focused on going to the customers. They took the game to Starbucks, Barnes & Noble, and Amazon.com. Without exception they were told, "We don't do games." They responded, "You're right, but this is more than a game. It's what your customers are really looking for." All three signed on.

Within the first six weeks they sold 10,000 games at a retail price of $34.95. In short order, *Cranium* became the fastest selling independent board game in U.S. history.

Alexander recalls, "We were driving around with games in our cars, restocking stores, staking out Barnes & Noble stores, monitoring how people were eyeing our game, how they were picking up the box. As the game took off we had to become masters of cash flow management, manufacturing, and forecasting. Because we had never done it before, we looked at everything and said, 'What's the best way to get this done rather than the historic way to get this done?'"

With all their success, Alexander laughs a bit nervously as he remembers the seminal moment he had to fess up to his dad about his great new venture—"Dad, I'm leaving Microsoft to do a board game."

# Vision Casting

### Alvin Toffler
*Author and Futurist*
*Toffler & Associates*

*If you look to the probable future, it
frequently blinds you to what is often much more
important and that is the improbable future. The
really big changes in history and in the
marketplace and in business and in the economy
and in finance, I believe all start out as being
highly improbable, unlikely, but with enormous
potential impact.*

For four decades Alvin Toffler has been shocking us with
insights into the future of the powerful waves and
undercurrents that will impact every aspect of our lives.

With his wife Heidi as his collaborator since their days as
university students in New York City, Toffler has authored four
blockbuster books that have had a worldwide impact, *Future
Shock, Third Wave, Powershift,* and *War and Anti-War.* These works
have sold millions of copies, have been translated into over thirty
languages, have added new words to dictionaries, influenced
corporate strategies, and impacted politics in various countries—
perhaps none more than the development of modern China.

Says Toffler,

> If I stand back and look at this as though I were a historian, looking back from the 22nd century, I think what I would say is that we've caught a look at a society (I'm speaking of the United States in this case) which has completed half or two-thirds of its enormous transformation from a blue-collar industrial age economy and society to a new form of world creation and a new form of society that comes with it. The itch of the Third Wave has not reached the majority of human beings on the planet. Because of the way these waves change, they do not spread evenly and they roll faster in some societies than in others and there are some communities and societies we can never reach.

Innovation and sustainable growth in the organization happen within the rich context of the broader forces. Understanding these forces, counter forces, crosscurrents, and global market opportunities requires a broad-based and fluid kind of vision that can see and interpolate the interrelationships.

# A Fine Disregard for the Rules of the Game

**Kirk Varnedoe**
*Professor of the History of Art*
*Institute of Advanced Studies, Princeton*

*You want to look at art for two things that intersect: Art steps outside your own timeframe, outside your own mortality. It gives you a sense of some enduring human spirit that goes beyond your lifetime; it connects you to humanity and to other humanities. At the same time you look to art for something that goes faster than you do, that goes faster than the seasons, that doesn't have a regular beat but surprises you, that innovates, that quickens your life and makes you more aware of being alive and connects us more to your own time.*

The eloquent and erudite Varnedoe is not what you might expect at the top of the pyramid in the refined world of modern art. I first heard him lecture at Columbia when I was a student, and he was simply the best lecturer I had ever heard. The hale and hearty Varnedoe used to ride his motorcycle to class, slaloming through the gridlock of New York City, quickly detoxifying the art experience for a whole group of freshman football players and wrestlers. A compact and muscular man, he had been featured on the cover of *Rugby Magazine* when we met last spring.

Kirk Varnedoe is one of today's clearest and most articulate thinkers on innovation and how the creative process works. Varnedoe's insights into the creative mind and the process of innovation are drawn from his knowledge of the disparate fields of art, physics, molecular biology, aerospace, Darwinian evolution, mathematics, pop culture, and. . . . Rugby.

Varnedoe recently left the New York Museum of Modern Art, where he had been the long-time chief curator of painting and sculpture, for a position at the prestigious Institute of Advanced Studies at Princeton, the legendary think tank that has been the home to Einstein, Oppenhimer, and dozens of Nobel Laureates and winners of the Wolf and MacArthur prizes and Fields Medal.

Recognized as one of the most important curators and art historians of the late twentieth century, Varnadoe has organized major retrospective exhibitions of the works of Jackson Pollock, Jasper Johns, and Sy Twombly, as well as historical examinations of the works of Van Gogh and Rodin. His exhibitions such as *High and Low: Modern Art and Popular Culture* represent the intersection of dialogues between modern art and advertising, graffiti, caricature, and comics. All were seminal events that continue to generate debate and admiration among artists, curators, and cultural critics.

# The Power Of Dialogue

**Daniel Yankelovich**
*Founder and Chief Executive Officer*
*Viewpoint Learning*

*The most gifted people make some of the biggest mistakes because they only see things from their own field of vision. Only dialogue is designed to dig beneath the surface of ordinary conversation and bring to light the diversity of people's views. Dialogue engages people at a more profound level of depth, openness and empathy. It is learning from these perspectives that shapes leadership, judgment, foresight and real understanding. Ultimately, we all come to a higher place through understanding others' points of view and broadening our own points of view.*

Dan Yankelovich is a compassionate man with great powers of observation, whose searching intellect misses nothing. His discoveries have pioneered entirely new ways for us to understand and know both the world and ourselves. In the exuberant garden behind T George's house in La Jolla, we settled into a full throttle conversation with him:

They say in science that most insights come from struggling with anomalies. That certainly was the way I came to my work on dialogue. There is this conventional picture of how people form judgments. It's the theory that the media experts operate under—the premise that you give people information and they make up their mind. They believe that if you have something that's difficult or controversial, you should present it through debate, which gives the listener or viewer both sides of the picture; and on that basis they make up their mind. It's a commonly held view; it's almost never challenged, and it has almost nothing to do with reality!

I began to realize that there is a powerful kind of knowing that comes from dialogue that does not come from more conventional categories of knowledge. It is way of knowing very different from the way of knowing based on expert information. It is a form of knowledge that comes from seeing and comprehending multiple viewpoints; and it holds the key to finding new creative approaches and developing and implementing inventive solutions. For most of us, learning has been associated with factual information, scientific research and technical expertise, not dialogue.

Yankelovich recently founded Viewpoint Learning. A visionary pioneer and famed social scientist, he is recognized as the leading interpreter of trends and forces shaping American society and the global economy. He is a prominent advisor to large corporations, universities, governments, communities, and presidents. His trail-blazing career in market research includes founding the New York Times/Yankelovich Poll; as well as sitting on numerous boards including CBS, U.S. West, Brown University, The Carnegie Foundation, and The Charles F. Kettering Foundation. He is also a Senior Fellow at the Kennedy School of Government at Harvard University, Special Advisor to the Aspen Institute, and has held Professorships at NYU and The New School.

## 13

# The New Silk Road

*If the doors of perception were cleansed everything would appear to man as it is, infinite.*

–William Blake

Like the great idea exchanges at the crossroads of cultures, from the ancient Athenian Agora to the cradle of the Renaissance in Florence to Wall Street in New York City, organizations must become dynamic creative centers where artists, architects, social scientists, entrepreneurs, futurists, poets, shaman, spiritual leaders, inventors, and creators of all types mix their art, science, cultures, and knowledge.

Great businesses are centers for ideas, the heartbeat of commerce and learning, the places where ideas, information, and first-hand access to diverse sources of knowledge across disciplines flow with ease and speed. Innovation must live, not only at an organization's periphery where the orthodoxies and control are the weakest, but in its core, at the heart of the organization itself.

The transition will not be easy. The move from an industrial mindset, in which business is involved with making things and selling things, to an Age of Ideas mindset, in which business functions as source of ideas and innovation, will require a complete re-imagining of the organization itself. It will require a full-scale recalibration of leadership, as well as of the structure of an organization. Because the arts are the language of the imagination, we believe they offer a ready source for businesses looking for new and better ways of thinking.

This will be the great challenge for a new generation of leaders: to envision the future of business in the Age of Ideas; to build new organizations that are designed to adapt to changing terrain; to creatively lead those enterprises into new areas in new ways; and to completely reconceive the economics of competitiveness around the knowledge worker.

Although we can only imagine the new forms organizations will take on in our evolving society, there is one *for sure* we must keep in our sights: the most important things we have to give are our love and our labor. Both the knowledge worker and the knowledge enterprise need to ask: *Is this an organization worthy of my labor? If we achieve our goals and our bottom line, so what? Has humanity been well-served?* To succeed in the future a company will have to be worthy of commitment.

> **Because the arts are the language of the imagination, we believe they offer a ready source for businesses looking for new and better ways of thinking.**

Most of us will spend the better part of our lives and waking hours at work—creating our living and our lives. How can we initiate a virtuous cycle to engage the hearts, minds, and hands of the people in our organizations? One that harnesses the beauty of the collective imagination at full throttle. A place where talents burn bright, rather than out.

It begins with the understanding that good management is an act of responsibility; it must be life engaging. It demands a kind of sacred trust in the care and well being of others. It requires a full measure of trust, compassion, integrity, grace, honesty, justice, and inspiration. And it is fueled by a level of vision and imagination we do not arrive at by default.

Organizations of the future will be grown from a well-discovered sense of purpose. They will be collaborative; they will respect and value the knowledge, interests, and skills of the individuals who give their labor; and they will be connected, based on real relationships and full-bodied exchanges.

Such an organization will be sustained by using the whole spectrum of imaginative tools.

---

### Tools for imaginative intelligence

- **Discovery** brings the vitality and virility of wonder to the organization. A new sixth sense and geyser of ideas.

- **Story** connects us to the most transformational knowledge in the organization and brings a powerful narrative that goes straight to the heart.

- **Conversation** allows us to move ideas forward and galvanize resources.

- **Contradictions** bring a fuller range of vision.

- **Voice** ignites the feeling of exhilaration, power and fulfillment when we connect and act with the fullness of our capacity.

- **Sketchpad** allows us to experiment intensively and find the furthest reaches of our ideas.

- **Space** facilitates communication and information flows, allowing the full scope of our knowledge to flow in and through it.

- And **generosity** multiplies them all, providing a radiant source of energy creation.

The time for these tools is now; the place is here; and the opportunity is unprecedented. American business has access to the greatest confluence of capital, knowledge, education, and information in the world. The result could be so much more than simply making things and selling things. It could be about transformation itself! What we are proposing is a new organizational model for personal and collective advancement of human progress itself. We are proposing genuine, extravagant, healthy growth.

# ACKNOWLEDGEMENTS

We could not have written this book without the friendship, support and advice of countless family and friends especially Sam, John, Rob and Kate Stephens, Sam Imende, Alex Zades, Lainie and Katie LaVacca, Philip Hanes, Jeannie Harris, Katie Holland, Anna Bolton, and Nicole Ryan. To anyone we have missed, we apologize in advance.

We would like to gratefully acknowledge the mad dogs, dreamers and sages for sharing their stories that so inspired us. Much of the light leaving them now won't hit the rest of us for a long time, and when it does we may not recognize its source. That's our best clue to its power.

To our friends at Elounda Press, we are grateful for your hard work, belief, and encouragement.

We would also like to thank the entire Sundance community for their generosity of spirit: Robert Redford, Michelle Satter, Ken Brecher, Patrick Hubley, Joan Darling, Stanley Tucci, Miguel Arteta, and Michael Lehman.

To the entire family at LHC, we shared a dream and saw it realized. A special thanks to the executive team for their leadership, friendship and for building a truly great agency: Mylene Pollock, Neil Saunders, Kate Holmes, Peter Mitchell, Joe Naparano, and Brad Bennett. A special thanks to Mike Foley who logged thousands of miles with us on this journey and in a moment of inspiration sparked the title of this book.

To Dr. Elizabeth Chiseri-Strater and Dr. Hephzibah Roskelly of University of North Carolina at Greensboro for their help in conceptualizing the study early on, to colleagues at Elon University and High Point University for helping to turn the ideas as we went, and to Nancy Olsen of Quail Ridge Books in Raleigh for her inimitable ongoing advice about good books.

A special word for our colleagues at Wake Forest University Graduate School of Management, Dean R. Charles Moyer, Kim Westmoreland, Ajay Patel, T. Vernon Foster, Michelle Roehm, and Melissa Combes for providing a wonderful forum for dialogue and for sharing their wisdom, experiences, and ideas.

Special thanks to Mary Bolton, Jean Corey, and Rita Pleimann for their good insights draft after draft, and to our families for running our lives in a way that made it possible to write this book, especially Arthur and Zelda Bowen and Stamos Zades.

Thanks to Fu-Ding Cheng for good karma and wonderful artistry and design, to Lloyd Whitehead and Darrell Bailey for keeping our computers and networks running through all the viruses and lightning storms.

And a final thank-you to Leigh Buchanan at *Inc.* magazine for seeing the possibilities in our work and for her skillful collaboration. To John Koten, Jane Berentson, and Kelly Winkler, Andrea Dunham, Alexandra Brez for their support and unique ability to get new stories to press.

# *Notes*

## 1 Growth in the Age of Ideas

[1] Gretchen Morgenson, "Earnings Are Worse Without The Icing," *Wall Street Journal* July 13, 2003, cites research by David Bianco. David Bianco, accounting analyst at USB, studied the results at each of the S&P 500 companies over the last 11 years, viewing earnings and accounting practices over an entire economic cycle. When he adjusted the companies' reported charges, stock option grants, and overly rosy pension assumptions, what he found was troubling. In 1991, the adjusted earnings were roughly 18 percent less than those the companies reported to shareholders, but by 2002, the difference grows more vast: *after being adjusted for the funny stuff, earnings were 41 percent less than the profits reported to investors*!

[2] David Henry, "After the Merger Hangover," *BusinessWeek,* October 14, 2002. *BusinessWeek*, in a study designed with Mark L. Sirower, head of Boston Consulting Group's M&A practice, examined 1,000 deals worth at least $500 million announced between July 1, 1995 and August 31, 2001.

[3] Toni Morrison, "The Site of Memory," *Sites of Invention: Inventing the Truth: the Art and Craft of Memoir*, Ed. William Zinsser (Boston: Houghton Mifflin, 1995), 85-102.

[4] Peter Drucker, "The Age of Social Transformations," *Atlantic Monthly,* December 1995.

[5] Peter Drucker, "The Age of Social Transformations," *Atlantic Monthly,* December 1995.

[6] Jim Collins and Jerry I. Porras, *Built to Last* (New York: Harper/Collins, 1994), 46.

[7] Peter Drucker, "The New Pluralism," *Leader to Leader*, No. 14, Fall 1999.

[8] B. F. Skinner as quoted in Alfie Kohn, *Punished by Rewards: the Trouble with Gold Stars, Incentive Plans, A's, Praise, and Other Bribes* (New York: Houghton Mifflin, 1999), 19.

[9] Alfie Kohn, *Punished by Rewards: the Trouble with Gold Stars, Incentive Plans, A's, Praise, and Other Bribes* (New York: Houghton Mifflin, 1999).

## 2    Discovering Imaginative Intelligence

[1]Howard Gardner, Professor of Education at Harvard University, has led breakthrough work in dismantling a singular IQ approach to intelligence. In his pioneer work, *Frames of Mind: the Theory of Multiple Intelligences* (New York: Basic Books, originally published 1983), Gardner identifies seven separate realms of intelligence that all individuals have: linguistic, logical-mathematical, spatial, musical, bodily, interpersonal, intrapersonal, and naturalistic. Gardner's understanding of intelligence focuses on the "stuff" we think with, the mental representations we use to learn, understand, and create knowledge.

Gardner himself acknowledges that there is no magic to the taxonomy of seven types of intelligence and his own understanding of them continues to evolve. His work has provided new terrain for many scholars in a variety of areas to explore a radically expanded notion of intelligence, among them, Dan Goleman (*Emotional Intelligence: Why It Can Matter More Than IQ* (New York: Bantam Books, 1994).

Goleman has stretched our sense of the power of emotional intelligence in a way that broke ground for our focused thinking about the power of imaginative intelligence. Whereas the basic assumption about traditional IQ was that there was little one could do to change it, Goleman believes that emotional IQ has greater impact on our relational and corporate lives—and, to a great extent, can be developed; so too with imaginative intelligence.

[2] Investopedia.com, "Organic Growth" and Baystreet.Ca, "Investment Glossary-Organic Growth.

[3] Warren Buffet, Berkshire Hathaway Inc. 2002 Annual Report, Chairman's Letter, 10.

[4] Penelope Patsuris, "All Eyes on the Interpublic's Client List," *Forbes.com,* November 11, 2002.

[5] T.W. Siebert, "Long Haymes Attracts Veteran British Planner," *Adweek,* August 2, 1999.

Vincent Coppola, "Cover Story-Welcoming Committee," *Adweek*, October 2000.

Jim Osterman, "Cover Story-She's In Charge," *Adweek*, March 1999.

[6]*Adweek*, "Agency Report Cards," April 7, 1997.

[7] Curtis Sittenfeld, "Report From the Future. The Creative Odyssey," *Fast Company*, October 1999.

Marcia Stepaned, "Tell Me a (Digital ) Story," *BusinessWeek*, May 15, 2000.

"Why the Hot Agencies Are Out of Town," *Time,* November 1996.

[8] T.W. Siebert and David Gianatasio, "Virgin Cola Moves Creative to Long Haymes Carr," *Adweek,* April 3, 2000.

9 Vincent Coppola, "Absolute Power," *Adweek*, November 13, 2000.

Vincent Coppola, "Dunlop Selects LHC," *Adweek*, October 23, 2000.

Vincent Coppola, "Long Haymes Carr Wins Advertising Account of Regional Carrier," *Adweek*, January 8, 2001.

Vincent Coppola, "Cover Story-Maxximum Return," *Adweek*, December 4, 2000.

10 Teresa M. Amabile, "How to Kill Creativity," *Harvard Business Review*, October 1998.

11 James T. Berger, "Creative Odyssey Keeps Winston-Salem Agency in the Big Game," *Business Life*, November, 2000.

12 Jane Secomb, "LHC Presents George Stephanpoulos," *Winston-Salem Journal*, August 6, 1999.

13 Bonnie Schwartz, "Report From the Future-Off the Walls," *Fast Company*, June 2001.

14 Mara Der Hovanisian, "Zen and the Art of Corporate Productivity," *BusinessWeek*, July 28, 2003.

## 3     The Odyssey Project on Imaginative Intelligence

1 Howard Zinn, *The People's History of the United States: 1492-Present* (New York: HarperCollins, 1999), 1-11

2 Warren Buffet, Berkshire Hathaway Inc. 2001 Annual Report, Chairman's Letter, 10.

3 Nelson Mandela as quoted by Anthony Sampson, *Mandela: The Authorized Biography* (New York: Vintage Books, 1999), 404.

4 As told by fellow prisoner Neville Alexander to John Carlin, *Frontline*, http://www.pbs.org/wgbh/pages/frontline/shows/mandela/prison/alexander.html

5 Cornel West in conversation at Elon University, March 19, 2003.

## 4     Discovery

1 Peter Drucker, "The Shape of Things to Come," *Leader to Leader*, Summer 1996.

## 5     Story

1 Thomas L. Friedman, *The Lexus and the Olive Tree* (New York: Farrar Straus & Giroux, 2000), 110.

2 The reasons why the benefits of the M&A process are rarely realized are described more fully in an article by David Henry, "The Merger Hangover- How Most Big Acquisitions Have Destroyed Shareholder Value," *BusinessWeek*, October 14, 2002.

3 Thomas Stewart, *The Wealth of Knowledge: Intellectual Capital and the Twenty-first*

*Century Organization* (New York: Utopia Ltd., 2001), 8.

[4] I visited *Daddy Jack's* in July 2002, post 9/11 and their business was as robust as ever.

# 6    Conversation

[1] Of course, in many ways the U.S. got it wrong from the beginning. Women had less access to strategic conversations, information, and ownership than men, and slaves and Native Americans had virtually none at all. Ironically these communities were devastated by colonists who wrote and fought for some of the most brilliant works of human dignity and independence ever written.

[2] We are using *America* and *American* here to mean the United States of America. The choice is imperfect and obviously slights our shared ownership of the name with Latin America, but we have chosen it over the ongoing use of the term "U.S." because it seems to hold more of the story and personality of the country for readers.

[3] Robert McNamara, *In Retrospect: The Tragedy and Lessons of Vietnam* (New York: Vintage Press, 1996) xix. Bill Hybels of Willow Creek Community Church first pointed me to this book. McNamara's use of first hand documents allows for a revealing rhetorical critique, which I developed in my unpublished dissertation, *Remembering Seems Wise: The Rhetoric of Women's Leadership (University of North Carolina at Greensboro,* May 2000), 141-150.

[4] A few years ago, with a colleague Dr. Jean Corey, I interviewed freshmen at our universities about their experiences of being read, misread, or read well by their high school teachers. We found that though the students knew intuitively what we meant by being read well by a teacher, many of them had never had the experience. Out of the hundred students we interviewed, twenty wrote about having an extraordinary teacher in high school who read them with insight and responsiveness, whereas forty-five said they had been significantly misread or misinterpreted by a teacher. Here's the most troubling part of the study, however: thirty-five of our one hundred students said they had never had a teacher give serious attention to reading them at all. Furthermore, the students in the last group, those that were unread, were far more disappointed by their teachers than the second group, those who were merely misread.

For further reading on this study see Iris Chapman, Jean Corey, and Jane Stephens, "Between the Lines: Reading and Misreading Student Writers," *Journal of College Reading and Learning,* Spring 2003.

[5] Cary Chemiss, ed. and Daniel Goleman, ed., *The Emotionally Intelligent Workplace: How to Select For, Measure, and Improve Emotional Intelligence in Individuals, Groups, and Organizations* (New York: Jossey-Bass, 2002).

[6] Yankelovich has served on diverse and influential boards, including CBS, Educational Testing Service (ETS), the Japan Society, the Fund for the City of New York, the Kettering Foundation, and Brown University. In the process he learned much about conversation.

Yankelovich rose to national prominence as one of the only Pollsters who correctly predicted the too-close-to-call 1960 election. When the national polls were showing a 50-50, Yankelovich found a group of citizens in Syracuse, NY with the same split. From his background in psychology he had developed a theory of "working through," the process of struggling with hard things and conflicting values. He had noticed that when people come up against something that is not easy to accept and absorb, like losing a job or going through a divorce, it takes a certain amount of time for them to work through the issue. It occurred to him that he might be able to arrange a dialogue to help a group of people to "work through" the hard decision-making process of choosing a President in a compressed time period. He spent an hour with the group and led them through a process of struggling with the pros and cons of each candidate. At the end of an hour, when he asked them who they would vote for, the changed minds netted out 52-48 in favor of John Kennedy, leading Yankelovich to predict a narrow victory for Kennedy in the national election.

7 We were fascinated by the healthcare dialogue project. Here's more on it from Yankelovich: "What's interesting is in the morning, before the dialogue begins we get people to react to the four choices we have developed as they would in a poll. And the four choices are very close together so you couldn't make a governmental decision based on the poll data. By the end of eight hours, the choices and their implications become more sharply defined.

## 8    Voice

1 Frederick Buechner, *Listening to Your Life*. Compiled by George Connor (San Francisco: HarperCollins, 1992).

2 Carol Gilligan, *The Birth of Pleasure* (New York: Alfred A. Knopf, 2002), 224.

3 Maya Angelou, *Wouldn't Take Nothing for My Journey Now* (New York: Random House, 1993), 11-12.

4 See Andrew Samuels, *The Political Psyche* (London: Routledge, 1993) for a discussion of applying Bruno Bettelheim's concept of the "good enough parent" to organizational leadership.

5 For a rich discussion of this phenomenon, see Robert Bly, *Sibling Society* (New York: Vintage Books, 1997).

## 9    Sketchpad

1 Peter Elbow in conversation at CCCC in Chicago, March 21, 2002.

2 Peter Elbow in conversation, Ithaca, New York, June 26, 2003.

## 10 Space

[1] Stanislaus von Moos, *Venturi Scott Brown & Associates -Buildings and Projects, 1986-1998* (New York: The Monacelli Press, Inc., 1999), 350.

[2] Bonnie Schwartz, "Report From the Future," *Fast Company,"* June 2000.

[3] Charlie Rose interview with Denise Scott Brown and Robert Venturi *(Charlie Rose,* December 17, 2001).

[4] In some ways, Scott Brown sees the architecture of change as more eternal than modern. "Think of a thousand-year-old stone memorial or temple building that has flowers on its porch—the flowers fade in a day and the stone goes on for thousands of years. In a way the communication on these buildings are like the flowers. The relationship is of that nature. It's always existed in architecture as elements working up against each other, now it combines with electronics."

[5] The *Melatonin Room* was one of the exhibits in the San Francisco Museum of Modern Art during the Intel Corporation's sponsored exhibition from March 3-July 8, 2001, entitled *010101: Art in Technological Times.* The exhibit was organized to explore the confluence of art and technology in the digital age.

## Part III Introduction

[1] These ideas were inspired by Mihaly Csikszentmihalyi, *Creativity* (New York: HarperCollins Publishers, 1996).

[2] Stephen H. Zades and Jane Stephens, edited by Leigh Buchanan, "Creativity Regained," as first published in *Inc.* by Gruner+Jahr USA Publishing, September 2003.

## 12 The Mad Dogs, Dreamers amd Sages

*An Elegant Cordee*
[1] Maurice Herzog, *True Summit: What Really Happened on the Legendary Ascent of Annapurna* (New York: Simon & Schuster, 2000).

[2] Charlie Rose interview with Denise Scott Brown and Robert Venturi *(Charlie Rose,* December 17, 2001).

[3] Charlie Rose interview with Denise Scott Brown and Robert Venturi *(Charlie Rose,* December 17, 2001).

*Embracing Contraries*
[1] Peter Elbow, *Embracing Contraries: Explorations in Learning and Teaching* (Oxford: Oxford UP, 1987), 284.

typos
ix, 5, 10, 22, 23, 40, 41, 53, 69, 73
75, 85?, 95, 98, 104, 115,

202, 203

Send to
Bob Stec
Michelle Lamb


Molly 63
Lex DH - The DH Story 66, 68,
Soul of the brand 97
Steve M, D + S Guide for the Entrepreneur
NYC Museum p. 120


Age of Ideas,
Imaginative intelligence
Generosity